WHY STUDY THE I CHING?

A BRIEF COURSE IN THE DIRECT SEEING OF REALITY

Volume Five
Researches On The Toltec I Ching

WILLIAM DOUGLAS HORDEN

3 + 4 :: 6 + 1 :: RETURN

RESEARCHES ON THE TOLTEC I CHING SERIES:

    Volume One: I Ching Mathematics: The Science of Change

    Volume Two: The Image and Number Treatise: The Oracle and the War on Fate

    Volume Three: The Forest of Fire Pearls Oracle: The Medicine Warrior I Ching

    Volume Four: I Ching Mathematics for the King Wen Version

    Volume Five: Why Study the I Ching? A Brief Course in the Direct Seeing of Reality

    Volume Six: The Open Secret I Ching: The Diviner's Journey and the Road of Freedom

    Volume Seven: The Alchemical I Ching: 64 Keys to the Secret of Internal Transmutation

    Volume Eight: intrachange: I Ching Chess

DELOK PUBLISHING, ITHACA

Copyright © 2017 William Douglas Horden

ISBN-13: 978-1543209679
ISBN-10: 154320967X

Dedicated To My Dear Allies

CINDY BLACK   ANDREA BUTJE   LINDA RUTH

Contents

Foreword 7

Introduction 9

1. Direct Seeing 19

    Formative Substance 24

    The Eight Senses 28

    Seeing Through 36

    The Shift 44

    Summary 46

2. Reality 47

    From Compass To Map 53

    Talismans 57

    The Dream Body 67

Conclusion 75

Afterword 77

Foreword

My teacher, Master Khigh Alx Dhiegh, was fond of saying that the I Ching addressed the two deepest desires of human beings: *magic and enlightenment*. And, he reasoned, it did so more directly and facilely than any other practice of self-realization.

As an I Ching Master, he held that the act of addressing the Oracle with a question, performing a ritual of manipulating yarrow stalks or coins, and receiving an answer from the Oracle was, by definition, an act of magic—and, he reasoned, the divinatory act lay at the very basis of the worldwide culture of shamanism.

As an initiate of the Sudden Enlightenment School, he like his predecessors held that the diviner's mind comes to emulate the Oracle's Mind, which resides in timeless stillness until it is stirred by a question to movement in the form of a spontaneous answer—and, he reasoned, this natural reversion to stillness amid spontaneous responses to circumstances formed the perfect seedbed for an individual's awakening.

Reasons enough, I suppose, to study the I Ching. Certainly, they sufficed for me initially and, after nearly 50 years of practice, I still find them the most succinct answer to the question. But my teacher trained me to carry the work forward into the next generation of study. It is a charge I hope to fulfill in some small measure with the present work.

A classical argument among I Ching researchers is whether it is intended to be a work of divination or a book of wisdom. I would argue that its original purpose was as a mirror to the world—a mind mirror—that reflected both inwardly and outwardly the archetypal pattern of nature and human perception. As such, the I Ching's images—in particular, its eight trigrams—constitute a coherent representation of the unitary, non-dual nature of the relationship between world and mind.

It is from this perspective that the present book addresses the question, "Why study the I Ching?" What are the deeper implications of the I Ching that warrant serious study spanning decades? How, in this case, does its symbology assist in our piercing the veil of appearances and communing with the reality behind? What is the modern mind to make of the ancient soul? Do technological marvels justify taking up a purely materialistic worldview? Are we not haunted by Plato's World Soul, calling us back to the wisdom of a living intelligence binding together the world that cradles us?

This book takes up the matter of the underlying reality, how to perceive it and how to participate in it authentically. It does so in the context of the I Ching's symbology, particularly its eight trigrams. From this, the reader may safely assume that this is not a beginner's book—however, the Introduction does carry readers all the way through the introductory philosophical and symbolic material of the I Ching, so the inspired beginner might feel equipped to track unfamiliar terrain. Those familiar with the I Ching may benefit from the Introduction as well, since my terminology and perspective may differ from the received version to which they are accustomed.

I have benefited from being trained and initiated by two formal teachers and several informal ones, matters covered in my other books. Those first-hand experiences are the primary source material from which I draw in my writing—by which I mean, I do not write hypothetically: the practice I outline here is one I have followed personally and found to fulfill its promise.

The I Ching is roughly translated as *The Book of Change*, so it should come as no surprise that more authentically participating in change ought to serve as a worthwhile purpose for the dedicated student's life. Like any tool, there are ethical considerations required of anyone into whose hands it falls. To be an actual *agent of change* within the world of manifestation, in other words, demands a heart-mind filled with benevolence and empty of ulterior motives—self-interest is a poison unless it is fully integrated into the common good. Platitudes and good advice aside, I place this material in public view knowing that it might be misused—but knowing, too, that there is already so much misuse of human potential that the good this practice might evoke warrants the risk.

May your path carry you all the way to the ecstatic life.

WDH
Delicias, Winter 2017

Introduction[1]

The I Ching[2] has been in continuous use for 3,500 years, perhaps longer. It has attracted the attention of more serious commentators than nearly any other book in human history. Although thought of conventionally as a divinatory instrument, its commentators have focused almost exclusively on its formative relationship to human nature and reality. So deeply embedded in the structure of human nature and reality is its own structure, indeed, that its greatest predictive act may well be itself: only now in relatively modern times can we see that it reflects two of the most consequential scientific fields of inquiry—binary mathematics, by which we communicate with computers, and genetics, by which we have begun the exploration of the genetic code.[3] How the I Ching's own structure, discovered thousands of years ago, could have anticipated these most modern technologies hints at the deeper mysteries of this most ancient science of change.

When we speak of the I Ching's structure, we are pointing at a system of symbols comprised of solid and broken lines traditionally thought of in terms of complementary poles, such as light and dark, firm and yielding, masculine and feminine, day and night, etc. This system is then extrapolated into broader cosmological forces, such as creative and receptive polar forces describing the seed of potential that finds full expression in the fruit of realized manifestation. The sun is creative in that it produces light, whereas the moon is receptive in that it receives and reflects light.

The solid line is called yang and the broken line yin. Yang lines are thought of as active and in movement, while yin lines are thought of as responsive and at rest. This activity of yang is one of setting things in motion, such as conceiving new life, where the responsiveness of yin is one of sustaining and nourishing, such as carrying in the womb and giving birth.

---

[1] Regarding footnotes: In an age where information is immediately accessible via online search engines, I find it anachronistic to cite specific sources. Notes here will provide relevant keywords to facilitate searches—a method that benefits the reader by resulting in multiple sources covering any differing interpretations of the facts.

[2] Also spelled Yi Jing. But since the classic works, such as the Wilhelm/Baynes version, used the older spelling—which was likewise followed by my own teacher, Master Khigh Alx Dhiegh—I find no reason to adopt a new spelling that may in turn be one day replaced by something even newer.

[3] Leibniz discovered binary mathematics around 1700 while being introduced to the work of Shao Yung (circa 1000). The 64 codons of the RNA messenger code are precisely reflected in the structure of the 64 hexagrams of the I Ching.

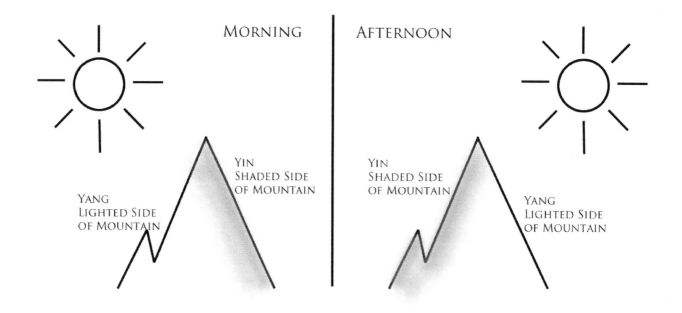

FIGURE 1: THE RELATIVITY OF YIN AND YANG

Neither are static states, however. They are relative to one another based on conditions and circumstances. This is so because they are complementary poles of *change*. The omnipresence of change establishes a universe of polarities: every unitary "thing" in other words incorporates its particular duality. The non-duality of all things, then, is identical to the duality of all things. This grounds the Taoist worldview squarely in an identification of Being and Nonbeing, Change and Nonchange, Appearance and Reality.

In Figure 1, above, we see that yang and yin are relative conditions in relationship to one another. In the morning, one side of the mountain is yang and the other yin, whereas they have exchanged positions in the afternoon. The circumstances of the mountain's verticality and the sun's movement combine to form two distinct characters whose presence is clearly felt in the lived experience of being on the mountain. Yang becomes yin. Yin becomes yang.

Because the I Ching is rooted in the animistic worldview, one in which all matter is invested with spirit (for how else could there exist an oracular spirit tied to the lines of the hexagrams?), the lived experience of the complementary polarities becomes an ever-increasing sensitization to the felt presence of their respective natures, characters, souls.

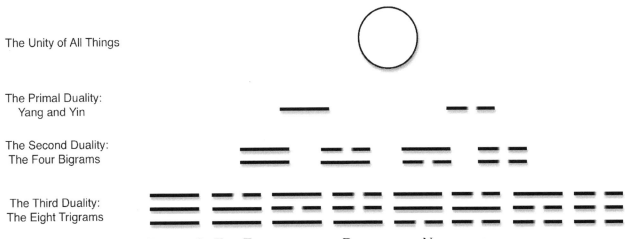

FIGURE 2: THE EMERGENCE OF BEING FROM NONBEING

Figure 2, above, presents the traditional way of depicting the Taoist worldview of I Ching cosmology. *The Unity of All Things* represents the non-dual nature of reality, which expresses the identification of Nonbeing and Being. Nonbeing is the unconditioned and timeless oceanic realm of living potential that is embodied in the unconditioned and time-bound oceanic realm of living manifestation making up Being. This is an identification summed up in the saying, *When Nonbeing moves, it is Being; when Being stays, it is Nonbeing*.

Once Nonbeing moves into Being, the primal duality of yang and yin arises. This appears to human senses as the polarity of Light and Dark, particularly embodied in the nature of day and night. Out of these two arise the four, particularly embodied in the four seasons of the year. And out of these four arise the eight archetypal images, particularly embodied in the eight compass points.

Figure 2 depicts the mechanics of symbolizing this progressive emanation into manifestation. The primal duality comprises a solid and broken line. They give rise to the four bigrams by (1) adding a solid line to the solid line, (2) adding a broken line to the solid line, (3) adding a solid line to the broken line, and (4) adding a broken line to the broken line. The eight trigrams are likewise constructed by first adding a solid line and then adding a broken line to each of the four bigrams in turn. Finally, the full entry into materialization is symbolized by squaring the eight trigrams to construct the 64 hexagrams.

From this straightforward progression of symbols there arises a relatively complex worldview of spatialized time. This is achieved by mapping the seasons of the year onto the four cardinal points of the compass. Generative energy (*ch'i*, *qi*) arises and begins things in the Spring/East; it waxes in the Summer/South, growing too strong and turns into its opposite in the Autumn/West, where it brings things to completion; it then wanes in the Winter/North, expending itself until there is nearly nothing left and again turns into its opposite in the Spring/East. Spring and Autumn are relatively stable spaces of time whereas Summer and Winter reach extremes that result in a re-polarization of generative energy and, subsequently, in its emanated manifestation.

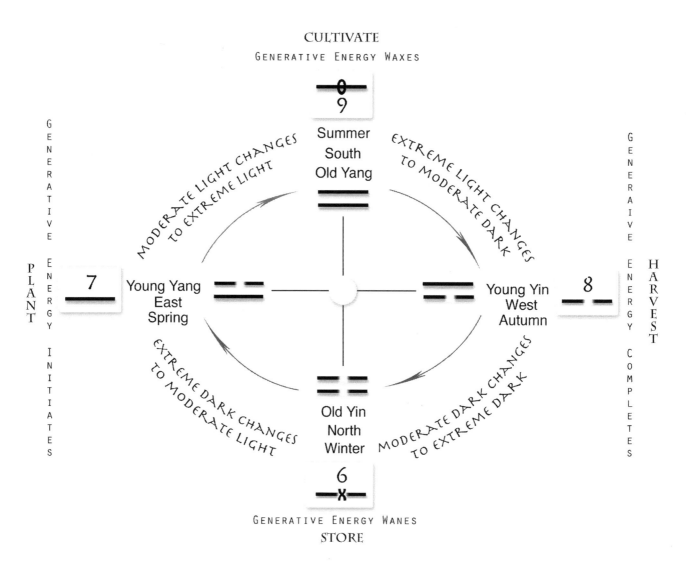

FIGURE 3: THE SPATIALIZATION OF TIME

The original primal duality of solid and broken lines is associated, then, with Spring and Autumn, while the more extreme Summer and Winter are associated with "changing lines" that transform into their opposite (solid line turns into broken line; broken line turns into solid line). This is symbolized in the corresponding four bigrams in that Spring/East (broken line over solid line) and Autumn/West (solid line over broken line) are both represented by a balanced combination of yang and yin ch'i, whereas Summer/South (two solid lines) and Winter/North (two broken lines) by an excess of yang or yin ch'i. These four spaces of time are particularly embodied in the Equinoxes and Solstices. The cyclic time binding such a worldview establishes the primordial strategy of human adaptability in the cycle of Planting-Cultivating-Harvesting-Storing, which generates strong metaphors in the psychological and spiritual spheres.

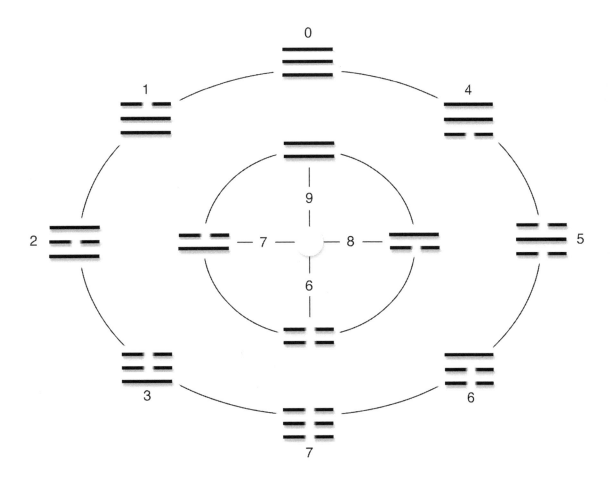

FIGURE 4: THE 4 BIGRAMS GIVING BIRTH TO THE 8 TRIGRAMS

Figure 4, above, is a straightforward depiction of the spatialization of trigrams from the bigrams, which is further elaborated in Figure 5, below.

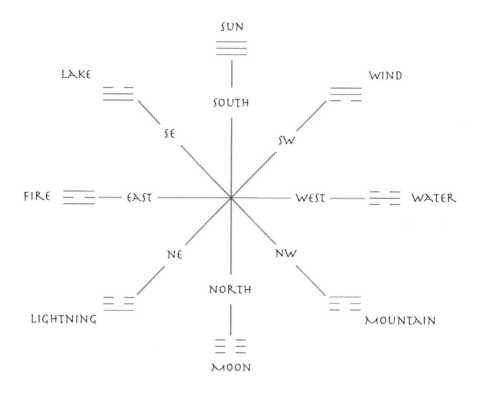

Figure 5: THE BEFORE HEAVEN ARRANGEMENT OF TRIGRAMS[4]

Arguably the best-known and most significant arrangement of the trigrams, the Before Heaven arrangement depicts the creative forces in perfect equilibrium *prior to* their entry into the world of manifestation. The Before Heaven arrangement of trigrams is a cyclic progression from creation to completion. Starting with *Sun*, the cycle moves counter-clockwise to *Lake* and *Fire* and *Lightning*, at which point it pivots across its axis to *Wind* and then descends clockwise to *Water* and *Mountain* and *Moon*—whereupon it pivots again across the vertical axis to *Sun* and begins the entire cycle over again.

---

[4] Readers used to previous versions of the I Ching will note slightly different nomenclature associated here with the trigrams—notably, *Heaven* and *Earth* are renamed here *Sun* and *Moon*, while *Thunder* is renamed *Lightning*. The use of the word *Heaven* is antiquated and confusing to Western readers. The name *Sun* here better conveys the creative, light-giving qualities of the trigram. Likewise, *Moon* better expresses the receptive, reflective qualities of the trigram than *Earth*. Beyond that, *Moon* is associated with the symbols for the tides, the womb, fertility and birth that convey the life-sustaining force of the great Feminine. It is worth noting that later Taoist alchemists found it necessary to add *Sun and Moon* to their repertoire of inner resources, associating them with the trigrams for *Fire and Water*. Both names, *Thunder* and *Lightning* convey the surprising, shocking and unexpected nature of the trigram—*Lightning*, however, is superior as a name, since the linear figure of the trigram depicts a lightningbolt (the light line at the bottom) falling from clouds (two dark lines above). Per Chinese tradition, South is placed at the top of the compass and East on the left.

FIGURE 6: THE ORDER OF COMPLETENESS

Figure 7 presents the eight trigram pairs *Sun-Moon*, *Lightning-Wind*, *Water-Fire*, and *Mountain-Lake* with their respective icons:

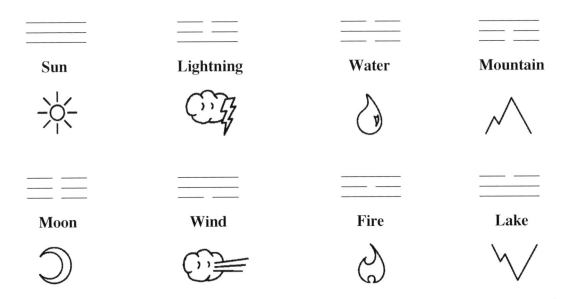

FIGURE 7: THE EIGHT TRIGRAM PAIRS

With this presentation, we can see clearly that each pair is comprised of trigrams whose three lines are precisely opposite one another (for example: the lines of *Water* are broken-solid-broken, whereas those of *Fire* are solid-broken-solid). This is what is meant by the Before Heaven arrangement standing in perfect equilibrium: each of its four pairs is balanced with its complement so that the entirety of the eight creative forces is held in abeyance, its creative potential the source from which all subsequent manifestation arises.

The final emanation is the result of squaring the eight trigrams in order to construct the 64 hexagrams.

The resulting Before Heaven sequence of hexagrams embodies every possible combination of *upper trigram* and *lower trigram*—

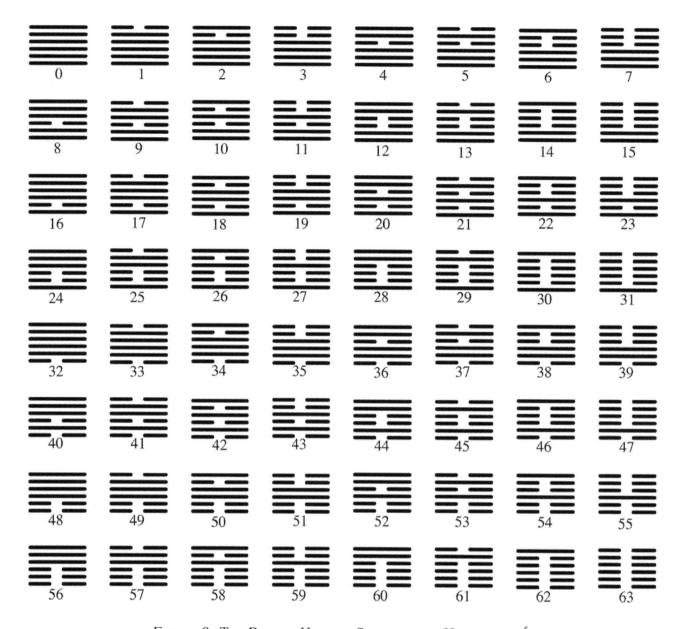

FIGURE 8: THE BEFORE HEAVEN SEQUENCE OF HEXAGRAMS[5]

A couple points are worth mentioning in regard to Figure 8. First, the Before Heaven sequence is also thought of as the natural number sequence, since it is precisely ordered according to the binary number

---

[5] Readers familiar with modern popular descriptions of the I Ching's binary code may be surprised to see here that the solid line equals 0 and the broken line 1. The opposite reading is based on the misconstruction by Leibniz, who was reading the order of the original Chinese upper-left to bottom-right, whereas it was written to be read bottom-right to upper-left. This correction was noted by Wilhelm himself and several others with the expertise to speak out, which has done little to stem the tide of popular misconception. The reading order has been adapted here for Western readers. This arrangement of hexagrams was first publicly revealed by Shao Yung.

of its hexagrams. Once solid lines are substituted with zeros and broken lines with ones, it becomes clear that the hexagrams actually *are* binary numbers.[6] Second, the hexagrams themselves depict archetypal situations due to their combinations of *Inner Trigram* and *Outer Trigram*, which constructs a symbolic language relevant to the possible permutations of internal state and external state (as relevant to an individual's inner state and outer circumstances as to a nation's domestic relations and international relations). Third, the *pattern* of upper and lower trigrams is such that the hexagrams in every *row* have the same lower trigram and the hexagrams in every *column* have the same upper trigram.

The remainder of this brief course in the direct seeing of reality makes extensive use of the background information presented above.

---

[6] See my *I Ching Mathematics: The Science of Change*

1. Direct Seeing

Generally, practitioners of the I Ching are most familiar with the hexagrams and possess only a passing familiarity with the trigrams. This is somewhat ironic, since the trigrams (pa kua, bagua) are the subject of intense study by practitioners of tai chi chuan, feng shui, traditional Chinese medicine, ch'i kung, and other traditional I Ching sciences.

Hexagrams arise from the interaction of the upper and lower trigrams. From this relationship, we can clearly see that trigrams are the fundamental elements of the I Ching's worldview.

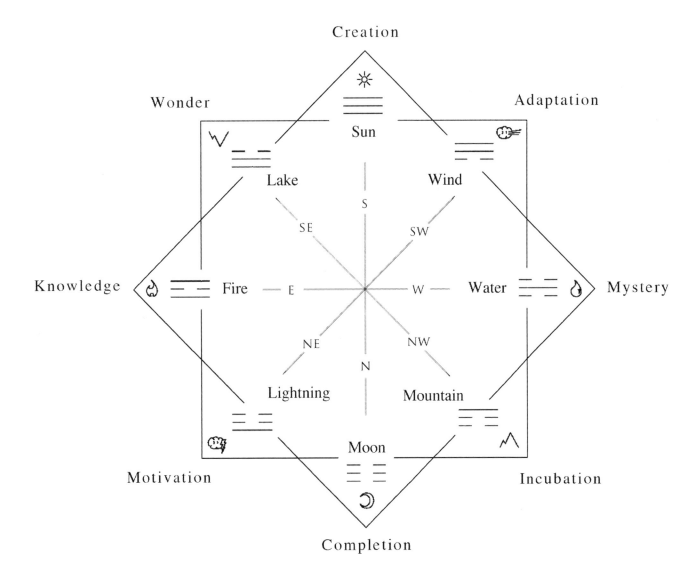

FIGURE 9: THE INNER COMPASS

Figure 9, above, carries us into the third stage of study of the trigrams by providing them with archetypal associations.

The first stage of symbolization is the pure three-lined image, constructed as shown in Figure 2, above.

The second stage is the association of each three-lined figure with an image of nature, per below:

☰ Three yang light lines represent the shining Sun

☷ Three yin dark lines represent the nighttime Moon

☳ Two yin dark lines above are clouds, one yang light line below is falling Lightning

☴ One yin fixed line below is the earth, two yang moving lines above is flowing Wind

☵ Two yin fixed lines are the banks of a river, one yang moving line between is rushing Water

☲ One yin dark line is empty within, two yang light lines outside are bright leaping Fire

☶ Two yin fixed lines below are the earth, one yang light line above is the sky-scraping Mountain

☱ One yin fixed line above is the earth, two yang moving lines below are the depths of the Lake

The third stage of symbolization is the association of archetypal meanings with their respective nature image (per Figure 9, above):

SUN ....**CREATION**: Initiating things, beginning things, starting projects or relationships, entering into something new. Making something new, discovering something new, uncovering new relationships between things. Sensing the essence of things, seeing the potential of things. An attitude of daring; adventuresome; delighting in exploration. Seed-thinking, consistent sowing of seed-intentions. Spirit as compared to Nature. Being as compared to Becoming, Essence as compared to Existence.

MOON .... **COMPLETION**: Finishing things, bringing things to completion, fulfilling the potential of things. Bringing projects or endeavors to full realization. The fruit as the fulfillment of the seed. Harvest as the fulfillment of sowing. Actualization, manifestation, embodiment. An attitude of nurturing and sustaining all things equally. Existence as compared to Essence; Becoming as compared to Being. Nature as compared to Spirit.

LIGHTNING ...... **MOTIVATION**: The surprising and unexpected events that incite movement. The impetus to break up inertia and stagnation. Volition, will power, sense of purpose. Intention. Crisis as a turning point. Shock of a trauma, as in the crash of thunder. Forceful suddenness.

WIND .... **ADAPTATION**: The gradual entry into things; gradual and deliberate resolution. Positive stubbornness; slow advance through impasses and barriers as tree roots penetrate soil and stone. Persistence. Patience. Unwavering flexibility to adapt to circumstances as wind flows around and through all obstacles.

WATER .... **MYSTERY**: The unknown aspect of events and things. The mysterious element that eludes explanation or solution. The uncertainty inherent to situations, endeavors and relationships. The element of risk accompanying endeavors as too little water brings drought and too much water brings flood. Deeper, immediate, intuitive knowing as compared to learned conscious knowledge. The unconscious as compared to the conscious.

FIRE .... **KNOWLEDGE**: The known, quantitative aspect of events and things. New learning. The intelligible and unambiguous element that is understandable and can be communicated. The certainty that is dependent on the five senses as fire is dependent on wood. The security sought in situations, endeavors and relationships. Past experience. Conscious knowledge such as that learned from familial and cultural influences. Superficial knowledge gained through social conditioning.

MOUNTAIN ...... **INCUBATION**: An interruption in the development of situations and things. A hiatus in the apparent development of something in order for a deeper level of advancement to occur. A period of gestation necessary for an idea, purpose or life to come to be fully realized. A period of tranquility, stability and contemplation. Setting apart as compared to gathering together. Symbolic death and metamorphosis as exemplified in the chrysalis.

LAKE.................**WONDER**: The sense of awe and astonishment arising from an open-minded and open-hearted appreciation of the miracle of being alive within the realm of manifestation. The sense of joy and excitement arising from being part of, and participating in, the uniting of spirit and nature. Communion with all of nature, human nature and spirit. Gathering together as compared to setting apart. Buoyant and light-hearted optimism. An attitude of sincere gratitude for the perfection of the world underlying its apparent imperfection.

The above list of attributes is by no means complete but it does express the nature of the trigrams well enough that serious students can expand it with associations based on their own first-hand experiences.

Figure 9, the Inner Compass, is, of course, based on the Before Heaven arrangement of the trigrams. As stated above, the Before Heaven arrangement is a cyclic progression from creation to completion. Its reading order establishes a visual pattern that implies the famous *yin-yang symbol* (t'ai chi tu, the Supreme Ultimate): Again, starting with *Sun*, the cycle moves counter-clockwise to *Lake* and *Fire* and *Lightning*, at which point it pivots across its axis to *Wind* and then descends clockwise to *Water* and *Mountain* and *Moon*—whereupon it pivots again across the vertical axis to *Sun* and begins the entire cycle again.

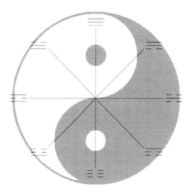

FIGURE 10: BEFORE HEAVEN SUPREME ULTIMATE

This reading order produces the *order of completeness* presented in Figure 6, above. It is duplicated here, below, followed by each trigram's association:

THE ORDER OF COMPLETENESS

SUN: The moment of inspiration that gives birth to a new endeavor.

LAKE: The initial excitement and enthusiasm that accompanies the beginning of a new endeavor.

FIRE: Gathering information and knowledge to further the endeavor.

LIGHTNING; Unexpected events or complications cast a surprising light on the endeavor.

WIND: Adapting the endeavor to the changing circumstances.

WATER: Hidden factors come to light, casting doubt on the viability of the endeavor.

MOUNTAIN: An interruption in the work during which the final form of the endeavor crystalizes.

MOON: Bringing the endeavor to completion, fulfilling its potential in accord with circumstances.

These are the eight archetypal operations, it is said, that make up the continuum of actions bringing the creative act all the way through to realization. Although the length of time of each operation may differ wildly—anywhere from mere seconds to entire decades—every endeavor follows this course of action. Needless to say, most endeavors are not carried through all the way to completion—the point at which they lose momentum can be charted precisely on the continuum of trigrams: a person remains stuck at the point of generating new ideas (Sun); or, remains stuck in the enthusiasm phase (Lake), never moving on to learning the things necessary to advance the endeavor (Fire); unexpected developments discourage a person from continuing (Lightning); a person refuses to adapt their original vision to changing conditions (Wind); previously unknown aspects of the situation increase the risks involved (Water); a person charges ahead toward the finish line rather than taking the necessary step back to allow things to coalesce outside conscious control (Mountain); or, at the end, a person loses the diligence and sense of caring needed to midwife the endeavor into the light of day (Moon).

Things move from creation to completion, in other words, not just according to these eight universal acts but *in this order*. It is as true for writing a book as it is for forming a relationship. And things fail to reach completion because people fail to accomplish the objective of one of the trigrams and so cut short the natural progression at that point.

The reading order of the trigrams culminates at the trigram Moon—*whereupon it pivots again across the vertical axis to Sun and begins the entire cycle again.* As is the case in every endeavor there is always the very real chance that reaching "the end" leads to another—often, higher-order—beginning. To finish one book may well lead to starting another. To find fulfillment in a relationship may well lead to a new cycle of mutual discovery and satisfaction.

To consciously make use of this order of completeness to manifest one's intention ultimately brings success. On the other hand, attempting to leapfrog over a phase in order to shortcut the progression is essentially the same thing as getting stuck in a phase—one's intention simply withers on the vine.

Formative Substance

Trigrams are considered to depict three coincident levels of experience, represented traditionally by their upper, middle and lower lines:

> ——— **Heaven**
> ——— **Man**
> ——— **Earth**

This ancient formula speaks to the fact that everything has two halves—a visible half, Earth, and an invisible half, Heaven. Human Nature, standing between these two poles, is comprised of both halves. The term *Heaven* signifies Spirit, while *Earth* signifies Nature. Nature is Form, Spirit is Formless and Human Nature is both.

> ——— **Spirit**
> ——— **Human Nature**
> ——— **Nature**

Trigrams, then, are tripartite symbols representing a unity that is essentially a duality yoked by a third, mediating, element.

Trigrams present, in other words, a coherent unity of three levels of progressive materialization, or emanation, ranging from the most ethereal to the most concrete. By way of example, we can point at the tripartite nature of water:

```
━━━━━   VAPOR
━━━━━   WATER
━━━━━   ICE
```

Water stands in the middle position between its solid, frozen, state and its vaporous, heated, state. What to call this unity? It is not strictly water. Nor ice. Nor steam. It is a single continuum of substance, the form of which changes as it changes density.

This is paralleled in ancient Taoist cosmology, wherein all things can be classified according to the density of their form:

```
━━━━━   SHEN
━━━━━   CH'I
━━━━━   CHING
```

Shen, Ch'i and Ching are the Chinese terms for the substance that has no form (Shen), whose form is palpable only to those sensitive to it (Ch'i), and whose form is perceptible to the five senses (Ching). From this standpoint, *Ching* is crystalized *Ch'i* and coincident with the living substance of the matter making up the entirety of the universe. *Ch'i*, likewise, is crystalized *Shen* and coincident with the living energy giving form to manifestation. *Shen*, the most ethereal substance, is the living spirit coincident with the creative intent of Pure Being.

The spiritual intent of the formless self-organizing principle (Tao) guides each thing from within. The generative energy of the Tao translates that formless intent into archetypal images of *formative substance*. The manifestation of the Tao materializes all the diverse individual forms of the archetypal images.

```
━━━━━   SPIRITUAL INTENT
━━━━━   GENERATIVE ENERGY
━━━━━   ANIMATE SUBSTANCE
```

This function of generative energy, as the translator of intention into manifestation, places its image-making urge precisely at that juncture of the formative process identified as the *pre-manifestation level*.

It is from this level of density that creative intent takes form as psychic images, gaining momentum to emerge at the correct time within the realm of manifestation:

INTENTION
PRE-MANIFESTATION
MANIFESTATION

It is no accident that the *pre-manifestation level* finds its analog in the *human nature level*. Rather, it is because human nature is an intrinsic part of Creation—one that serves the specific purpose of imaging just those forms of substance and their relationships that further the progressive development of the universe into its completed and perfected form.[7]

SPIRIT
HUMAN NATURE
NATURE

This brings us full circle back to the *order of completeness*, illuminating the mechanism by which its trigrams embody the spirit of progressive materialization.

Keeping in mind that a yang, solid, line signifies a *potential* state and a yin, broken, line a *realized* state, we can see that the sequence of trigrams depicts a sacred vessel being progressively filled by a sacred elixir.

Tracing the lines of potential and realized energies as they fashion the trigrams step-by-step provides a telling glimpse into the heart of the formative furnace.

---

[7] As an intrinsic part of Creation, human nature cannot be wholly coincident with *human beings*, a species that has only appeared in relatively recent times. Human Nature, on the other hand, is coincident with the inception of the universe: it is an immaterial awareness responsible for producing the imaginal forms in the pre-manifestation realm. In this regard, human nature is coincident with *Psyche* in the Neo-Platonic schema of cosmological emanation:

NOUS
PSYCHE
MATERIA

Human nature, therefore, pervades the universe throughout its complete cycle of creation-to-completion. Obviously, one of the archetypal images human nature has produced and brought to manifestation is that of human beings. The terms *Psyche, Soul,* and *Human Nature* are interchangeable.

| CREATION | WONDER | KNOWLEDGE | MOTIVATION | ADAPTATION | MYSTERY | INCUBATION | COMPLETION |

THE ORDER OF COMPLETENESS

CREATION: An entirely empty vessel, filled with infinite potential; the source of creative power

WONDER: Spirit realized; Human Nature and Nature in potential

KNOWLEDGE: Human Nature realized; Spirit and Nature in potential

MOTIVATION: Spirit and Human Nature realized; Nature in potential

ADAPTATION: Nature realized; Spirit and Human Nature in potential

MYSTERY: Spirit and Nature realized; Human Nature in potential

INCUBATION: Human Nature and Nature realized; Spirit in potential

COMPLETION: An entirely full vessel, filled with infinite realization; the womb of manifestation

We see here the substance behind form. The way that the Great Duality (yin and yang, broken and solid lines) expresses itself begins long before its forms ever become manifest. From absolute potential, it begins with Spirit and then works it way in combination with Human Nature down into Nature, with which further combinations of Spirit and Human Nature result in absolute realization. In the first four trigrams in the *order of completeness*, in other words, the realm of Nature is in potential, while in the last four trigrams the realm of Nature is realized: the first half of the creation-to-completion formative process occurs outside the realm of Manifestation, the second half within the realm of Manifestation. This can be understood in analog to the light from distant stars—even if it hasn't reached us yet, the light from a star hundreds of light-years away has already been radiated and is on its inevitable way to us. Spiritual Intent and Human Nature set in motion that which inevitably reaches Manifestation.

Each trigram represents a distinct distribution of *formative ch'i*.[8] No trigram is a complete image of reality. It takes all eight trigrams to depict the coherence of archetypal change. The Before Heaven

---

[8] The term *formative ch'i* stands for the entire tripartite entity *Shen-Ch'i-Ching* (Spiritual Intent-Generative Energy-Animate Substance), just as *Water* is understood to include all the phases of its tripartite nature (Vapor-Water-Ice). The Ch'i level itself (Generative Energy) is synonymous with *Formative Substance*.

arrangement is a mandala of wholeness embodying the eight possible allotments of the creative and sustaining forces circulating among and within all things in all times in all places. The *order of completeness* presents the natural movement of *formative substance* as it circulates among the trigrams, beneath the surface, so to speak, of the apparent static equilibrium of the four pairs of complementary-opposite trigrams.

Once we gain intimacy with the associated attributes of the trigrams, we begin to see the deeper implications of the ancient saying: *No Inside, No Outside*.

THE EIGHT SENSES

When a bubble bursts, what has changed? After all, it is the same air inside the bubble as outside the bubble. The membrane making up the surface of the bubble is the most tenuous and ephemeral of veneers, ever on the verge of bursting and reuniting the inside and outside air.

Though it may not be so all the time, there are moments in most people's lives when that surface is suddenly seen for the mirror that it is—a mirror reflecting the apparent inner and outer worlds in a vision of the nonduality of reality. And certainly, at the moment of death, the membrane of individuality dissolves as the river of subjectivity surges back into oceanic oneness.

It is axiomatic that our senses must be made of the same stuff as the world they perceive. This results in a good "fit" between perceiver and perceived, since the very substance of the five senses is identical to the substance of the universe—there is an already-existing predisposition toward perceiving the forms of the world since those forms share the underlying structure and function of the senses. In other words, the five senses are, themselves, forms of the world: *forms of the world perceiving forms of the world*.

But a good fit is not a perfect fit. We cannot hear subsonic sounds. We cannot see x-rays. Insects can see ultraviolet light we cannot and dogs can detect odors far out of our range of smell. Butterflies taste with their feet and the praying mantis can hear only one sound wave—the flutter of bat wings. Obviously, life forms adapt their senses to their survival needs. We do not need to see x-rays, so we don't. The praying mantis doesn't need to hear any other sound but the approach of its night predator, so it doesn't. The senses are, in this sense, filters, restricting sensory information to that which is necessary and useful for species survival. Yet, even within a species there are perceptual oddities:

caterpillars have such poor eyesight that it is highly unlikely that they could ever perceive a butterfly flitting nearby, let alone recognize it as *self*.[9]

Higher-order intelligence has allowed us to develop instruments that extend the range of the five senses. With telescopes we can see nearly back to the point at which the universe began. With electron microscopes we can see far into the microscopic world hidden from normal vision. And with reasoning based upon these extensions of our senses we can envision the makeup of the universe, contemplating what an eleven-dimension universe looks like or how parallel universes might interact within a multiverse.

It is this capacity of the imagination—to create an inner landscape more accurately resembling reality than the one generated by the five senses—that establishes the common ground upon which meet ancient mystics and modern researchers. Although the word "imagination" came to mean "mere daydreaming" in many circles in the West, that perception has been changing over the past few decades. Imagination is increasingly seen as the primary element of experience. Psyche itself is being more clearly seen as *images* and the classical meaning of *psyche*, as *soul*, is being understood as the deep connection individuals have with the *World Soul*. In this emerging worldview, which harkens back to earlier non-European cultures, there exists another world beyond the five senses which is accessed via creative imagination.[10] It is important to note that that other world is as real as this world, which implies an equally profound relationship between imagination and experiencing this world.

That other world has been termed the *Imaginal* in the West; it is called *Dreamtime* among the aboriginal peoples of Australia, the *alam al-mithal* by the Sufis, the *Pure Land* by the Buddhists, and the *Nagual* by the descendants of the ancient Toltec tradition of Mexico. My teacher, Master Khigh Alx Dhiegh, called it the *In-Between World* and considered it coincident with the *World Soul*.

All these cultures have long had sacred technologies by which they enter, and participate in, that other world. In I Ching sciences, that sacred technology is rooted in the eight trigrams.

---

[9] Which raises the question of whether we ourselves have the sensory capacity to perceive metamorphosed beings, let alone recognize them as *self*?
[10] See my *In the Oneness of Time* and *Way of the Diviner*.

In the same way that the bodily senses are made up of the same substance as the material world they perceive, the soul's senses are made up of the same substance as the Imaginal world they perceive.

The urimagination[11] *is* images. It perceives images, it produces images, and it consists wholly of images. The closest thing the modern mind can conceive of in this light is dreaming: in dreams, all one is doing is perceiving and producing images—yet those images, those symbols, convey emotions, thoughts, sensations, even memories. They are *living images*, in other words, that carry with them such a repertoire of effects.

Dreams are good analogs because nearly everyone has had profoundly significant dreams, the images of which elude rational interpretation and transcend the body's previous experience. The problem with the word *dream* is the same as with the word *imagination*—there are different levels of both, one superficial and the other profound. Some dreams are merely products of the body's experiences and others are clearly products of the soul's experiences. It is, of course, the latter that grant the body entry into the realm of living images, even if it is dependent on the conscious mind being asleep first. All this points to the dual nature of the *dream body*.

From the perspective of the body, the soul is the dream body. From the perspective of the soul, the body is the dream body. The difference between the two is that the body must be asleep to experience the soul as the dream body, whereas the body must be awake for the soul to experience it as the dream body.

For "the soul to experience the body as the dream body" means that *the soul grants the body entry into, and participation in, the other world*. This the soul accomplishes by sensitizing the body to the soul's eight senses.

The trigrams are the eight senses of the soul. The images they embody are the living symbols of the *pattern of perception* bridging the world of the five senses and the Imaginal world. They allow the soul to perceive the world of the five senses, even as they allow the body to perceive the Imaginal world. They are the images produced by the urimagination, the images perceived by the urimagination, as well

---

[11] I reluctantly coin this word to denote the primal imagination, the original psyche (prior to bifurcation into conscious and unconscious elements), that is the individual embodiment of the Imaginal world (as the individual soul stands in relation to the World Soul). It is intended to make avoiding the word "imagination" possible, as its connotations are misleading. The term combines the word *imagination* with the prefix *ur-*, meaning *primitive, earliest, original, first.*

as the senses themselves of the urimagination. They are the *urimages*, the archetypes, of the soul that make it possible to enter *either* world as a participant—for it is the urimagination that conceives both worlds in its role as co-creator with the *formative substance* itself.

Within the world of the five senses, these images depict the eight grand archetypal forces of Nature. Within the Imaginal world, these images depict the eight grand archetypal forces of Spirit.

From Figure 7, above. The trigrams with their associated archetypal images:

The eyes are not one of the five senses. They are a sense organ. The ears are not one of the five senses. They are a sense organ. The same with the nose, the taste buds, the skin. They are sense organs. The actual senses—sight, hearing, smell, taste, touch—these are the five senses of the body, mysterious bridges between the sense organs and the nervous system that the urimagination integrates into a cohesive, coherent *world of time and space*. Which is to say, a *world of experience*. A *world of meaning*. We know the universe we inhabit is actually a sea of subatomic particles, some denser in places and less so in others. Our bodies themselves are temporary bundles of subatomic particles in constant interaction with the surrounding temporary bundles of subatomic particles. Like the planet and the sun and the moon and the stars. Even the apparently empty spaces between stars is comprised of subatomic particles. People, animals, plants, minerals, mountains, rivers, everything: all temporary bundles of subatomic particles. But we do not experience the universe as temporary bundles of subatomic particles. We experience the universe as a cohesive, coherent world of time and space—not because of the five senses but because of the power of the urimagination to directly see the synergistic reality of the *formative substance*, the whole of which is greater than the sum of its parts. The soul's attention is drawn to holistic entities—especially to the web of relationships between its parts, rather than to the parts themselves.

To say that the trigrams are the eight senses of the soul is to say that the soul does not experience the world of the five senses as an accumulation of the five senses but, rather, as an accumulation of *meaning*. It is impossible to speak about images without speaking about meaning: one has a dream of a balloon floating along the ocean floor—each image, balloon-floating-underwater-depths-etc., becomes a meaning-laden symbol echoing personal and universal associations of emotion, thought, memory and sensation. The *meaning* of the dream, however, emerges not from the parts of the dream but from the whole event. And its meaning may well change over time for the dreamer—and, moreover, its meaning almost certainly appears quite differently to the dreamer who experiences it and others who hear of it second-hand. But all this extends well beyond dreams into ordinary waking life. A small group of hikers approaches a mountain: one person sees something to be overcome, another sees something to go around, and yet a third person sees a sacred place joining heaven and earth. A mountain may be the most solid and enduring of things, yet it is an ephemeral image, the symbolic content of which the soul both perceives and produces. The symbolic content of the mountain is a *living meaning* because it is the invisible half of a *living image*: it is neither static nor dogmatic because it is constantly changing as perception becomes ever more sensitive to the essential, archetypal, *formative substance* being manifested. Such perception increasingly integrates what the ancient Taoists called *appearance and reality*.

My teacher, Master Khigh Alx Dhiegh, often said, *People differ only in their sensitivity to the One*. This statement is the result of direct seeing of reality—and its integration with the surface of appearances in the psycho-social sphere. *Yes, people appear to differ. But that differing is the result of changing—and changeable—degrees of sensitivity to the Universal. And since that sensitivity is changeable, it does change, inevitably bringing all into full sensitivity of the One. Therefore, ultimately, people do not differ.* From such a perspective, neither appearance nor reality are ignored. Rather, they are fused into a single first-hand experience of image, sense, and meaning that unite the apparent contradictions of the past, present and future with the constancy of the timeless sphere.

It is the urimagination, the soul, that stands at the crossroads of image, sense and meaning.

——— MEANING
——— SENSE
——— IMAGE

By cultivating the soul's sensitivity to the unifying reality behind the diversity of appearances, we not only participate more meaningfully in this world of the five senses but also break through the perceptual barrier holding us back from entering the other world of the *Imaginal*.

From Figure 9, above: representing the archetypal attributes of the trigrams in the form of a mandala:

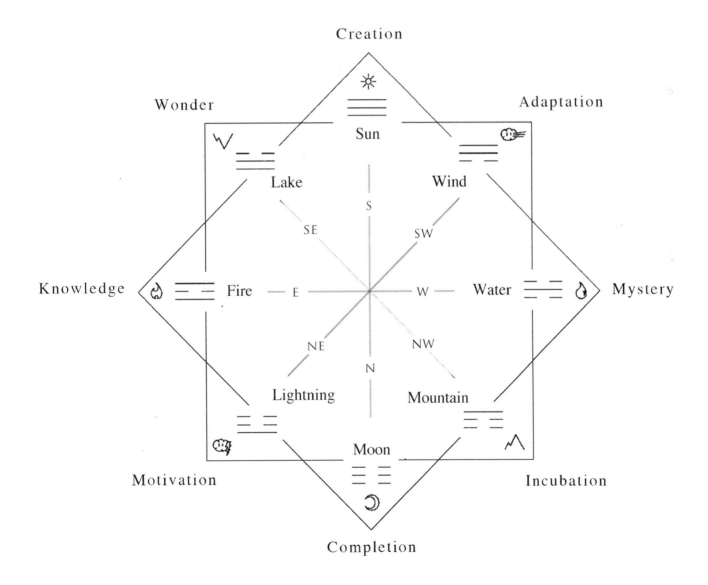

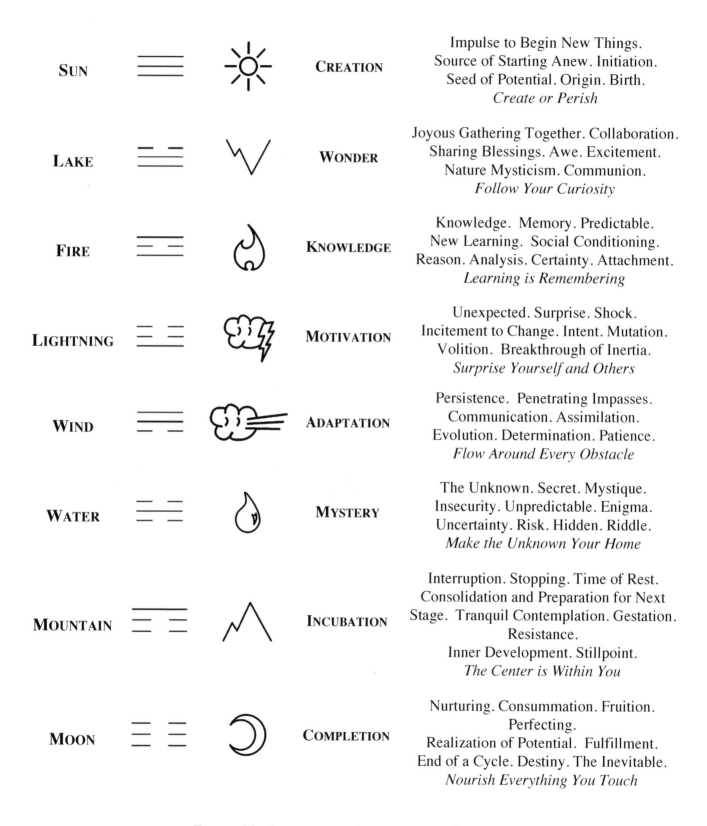

FIGURE 11: ARCHETYPAL ATTRIBUTES OF TRIGRAMS

Looking at a pond, it seems as though white clouds float on its surface. It is not that one cannot peer into the depths of the pond—but it is made more difficult by the sky's reflection. It is necessary to consciously adjust one's focus in order to *see through* the surface reflection and make out the bottom of the pond.

So it is with the direct seeing of reality.

This world of the five senses is the gateway to the Imaginal world. Beneath the surface of appearances, there is an underlying reality that gives form to this world of the five senses. True, the glare of sight, sound, touch, smell and taste nearly blinds us to the hidden depths of the world. But by consciously adjusting our focus—perceiving through the soul's senses—we are able to *see through* the surface appearances of the relative world and plumb the depths of the absolute world.

We "adjust our focus" by shifting our attention from the foreground to the background of awareness. Rather than having our attention habitually drawn to the objects of the five senses, we consciously turn our attention to the archetypal *formative substance* orchestrating their manifestation.

This entails recognizing the soul's eight senses and allowing what one is experiencing to register on those senses. This is a matter, somewhat paradoxically, of concentration and openness. Concentration in the same sense that one might be in a room where music is playing and so "hearing" it as background noise—then, suddenly aware of the music, one concentrates on it, bringing it to the foreground of attention. Neither the volume of the music nor one's proximity to its source has changed, yet one is immediately "hearing" it more loudly and more clearly. Focusing on one of the five senses like this is a combination of opening that sense to register a wider sensitivity even as one narrows attention by concentrating on that sense to the exclusion of the others.

Moreover, just as an experience at the beach, for example, might actively engage all five senses of the body, its underlying *formative substance* might activate multiple senses of the soul. Indeed, while most experiences trigger one or two primary trigrams,[12] there are exceedingly few experiences that do not evoke some aspect of each of the eight senses.

---

[12] We use the names of the trigrams (Sun, Moon, etc.) because no single associated term captures the full range of the archetypal attributes of the soul's senses.

Seeing Through

Just as some species cannot perceive something unless it moves,
Human beings cannot perceive something unless it changes.

The human body has five senses, the soul has eight.

The five senses depend on *difference*, on change, for perception. Silence changes to sound, day changes to night, hot changes to cold, sweet changes to bitter, pungent changes to fragrant. Standing, sitting, walking, or lying down, the body dwells in a world of change and has no conscious experience of the unchanging. Change is all the body knows, all the five senses can perceive.

The soul's senses, on the other hand, depend on *sameness*, on the unchanging, for perception. *All things change, nothing perishes.*[13] It is this *imperishable* that poets, musicians, artists, mystics and shamans have invoked for millennia. The world of change is the world of time, which, as has long been noted, is the world of birth and death. The imperishable is the deathless, the indestructible, the eternal, the timeless: it is the unchanging ocean out of which waves of change rise and into which they return. It is the One, the world of non-differentiation, the original unbroken sameness of the *formative substance* out of which all form arises and into which all form returns.

To see through appearances is a matter of *open concentration*—open sensitivity to the sense upon which one is concentrating. For example, one is in the midst of childbirth. The body's senses, of course, are nearly overwhelmed with physical sensations and all that is going on around one. Here one is deeply enmeshed in the world of birth and death. The world of time and change. Yet, one has simultaneously entered the timeless realm, participating in an archetypal ritual of the soul's contribution to the World Soul. Shifting one's attention from the body's senses to the soul's senses, the reality shining beneath appearances emerges in a series of overlapping visions of archetypal moment—

> SUN: An open window onto omnipresent radiance, light pouring into an atmosphere charged with the sense of an imminent birth; a new life entering Creation; an angelic being of infinite potential taking material form;

---

[13] Ovid, *Metamorphoses*

LAKE: Awe and wonder flood the heart in communion with all other souls waiting to greet the newest soul; spiritual joy and rejoicing in being part of the eternal act of universal renewal;

FIRE: Carrying the torch of preparation, learning and collective experience into the shadows of pain and disorientation;

LIGHTNING: Sudden paroxysms of awareness contracting into single points of explosive light;

WIND: Persistent and determined passing through an ordeal;

WATER: Standing on the threshold of the Unknown, coming face-to-face with the Great Mystery;

MOUNTAIN: A sure and certain break in the continuity of experience; inescapable aloneness in the performance of one's accepted duty; utter calm at the stillpoint of perfectly balanced tranquility and exaltation; spirit incubating inside the chrysalis of gestation;

MOON: The depths of the golden sea casting its treasure up onto the silver shore, fulfilling its sacred role in the destined perfection of Creation; the divine midwife ushering a new soul into the realm of absolute freedom; ripened fruit falling from the Tree of Life.

As stated above, there are experiences that activate at least some aspects of each of the soul's senses. An experience like childbirth certainly triggers aspects of all eight senses, while others activate as few as one or two. The matter at hand is the degree of *open concentration* that a practitioner brings to each moment.

Those who have practice in sensitizing themselves to their eight senses will have read the above descriptions of the activated trigrams and found their own senses activated—an experience called sympathetic, or resonant, urimagination. A higher degree of open concentration like this allows practitioners to resonate with the perceptions of others, sympathetically perceiving their own personal associations to the shared archetypes. The experiences of other souls, in other words, does not create identical experiences for the practitioner but does provide a springboard, so to speak, by which a corresponding archetype may be experienced. The capacity to perceive another's experience arises from one's openness, but the capacity to follow that into one's own experience arises from concentration.

The ancient advice is to *Start with what is close at hand*. This means that practitioners already have elements in their lives that may open the window onto the archetypal experience. Let us say that one can spend time with an infant, or a puppy, or a kitten, and so forth—*seeing through* surface appearances, one finds the joyousness of LAKE coming into focus, the full force of its *formative substance* pouring forth into manifestation. Here, the matter is the degree of one's openness, since it is easy to mistake the playful joy exhibited by the infant or puppy or kitten for the archetypal joyousness and wonder of LAKE.

The archetype, in other words, is using the form of the infant or puppy or kitten to pour forth its *formative substance* in a measure far greater than the form can ever contain. The greater the openness of one's sense, then, the more profoundly the corresponding archetype reveals the full range of its attributes. To speak of openness or sensitivity of the soul's senses is to recognize that it is the soul itself that allows itself to experience reality ever more profoundly, ever more meaningfully, ever more reverentially. To approach the divine with thinking or rationality instead of reverence is to remain wholly in the world of the five senses and continue to dull and obscure the soul's senses. To *start with what is close at hand* does not, therefore, mean that one approaches familiar people, places or things with a sense of already knowing them and simply looking to appreciate them more—anyone should be able to do that and, indeed, ought to. But that has nothing to do with seeing through appearances and encountering reality.

The second step is to work with the natural images of the trigrams, sensitizing oneself to the archetypal experiences they lay bare:

> SUN shatters darkness, dawn awakens promise
>
> LAKE attracts community, communion fosters joy
>
> FIRE depends on wood, knowledge depends on experience
>
> LIGHTNING strikes unexpectedly, surprise provokes change
>
> WIND flows without ceasing, flowing adapts to every impasse
>
> WATER rushes downward, the hidden follows the unknown
>
> MOUNTAIN stops movement, incubation transforms extinction
>
> MOON completes its phases, completion fulfills promise

It is useful at this stage of practice to spend time in the presence of the natural elements corresponding to the trigrams: sit in the sun, walk along the lake, stare into the fire, watch the lightning, stand exposed to the wind, lay beside the waterfall, climb the mountain, bathe in the moonlight. By concentrating on the trigram attributes while in the physical presence of their respective natural elements, one can sense the underlying reality shining through appearances—because the magnitude of the *formative substance* is many times greater than the natural element it manifests, the purity and meaning of the archetype shines through with an intensity that redoubles and redoubles again the reverence one experiences in every such encounter.

"Seeing through" means *Seeing the soul of things.*

This is exemplified in the list of formulas above. For example, where we read "SUN shatters darkness, dawn awakens promise," we can see that the first part of the formula (SUN shatters darkness) refers to the natural element, whereas the second part of the formula (dawn awakens promise) refers to seeing the soul of the manifestation. This is called, *Seeing the sun within the sun.*

The same holds true for the other seven formulas. "LAKE attracts community" refers to the natural element, whereas "communion fosters joy" refers to seeing the soul of the manifestation. This is called, *Seeing the lake within the lake.*

And so on, with each formula. *Seeing the fire within the fire. Seeing the lightning within the lightning. Seeing the wind within the wind. Seeing the water within the water. Seeing the mountain within the mountain. Seeing the moon within the moon.*

In each case, the soul of the natural element radiates a *charismatic impact*[14] of far greater magnitude than the manifestation's impact on the five senses. This is, first and foremost, because it is a soul-to-soul encounter: one's soul perceives the soul of the manifestation and, in a spontaneous act of communion, is granted entry to the full range of the archetype's *ancestral memory*.[15] From this standpoint, the archetype is said to possess a memory because of the way its many meanings are linked by association in a web of images assimilated and reinforced over the endless expanse of time.

---

[14] I use this term to designate *a divinely bestowed power or influence,* which harkens back to the original meaning of the word *charisma (grace).*
[15] I use this term in the sense of *the collective meaning of universal experiences vested in one of the soul's archetypes and open to recollection.*

To enter an archetype's memory is to step across a threshold of fixed and certain individuality and into a landscape of living images imbued with the indelible experiences of universal Human Nature. These are living images in the same way that the images in one's dreams are living aspects of one's own psyche. In this case, however, the dream is not one's own and the threshold one has crossed is the entryway into the universal *dream space* of the original urimagination. Whether called the Imaginal, the Dreamtime, the Nagual, or the World Soul, the objective reality of this dream space is unquestionable once experienced. Encountering living images within the dream space, practitioners come to recognize that they themselves are likewise living images—and, likewise, living aspects of the timeless dream of the universal psyche.

This dream space is the objective reality of the *formative substance* that uses archetypal images to translate pure idea into physical manifestation. Such a translation is possible because the soul's senses are intrinsically attuned to the archetypal images of the *formative substance*.

Figure 12, below, presents the archetypal senses in the order of completeness:

TRIGRAM	URIMAGE	SENSE
Sun	Some Make Things	Generating
Lake	Some Are Pulled To Things	Attracting
Fire	Some Find Things	Showing
Lightning	Some Move Things	Surprising
Wind	Some Move Through Things	Adapting
Water	Some Veil Things	Hiding
Mountain	Some Stand Apart From Things	Distancing
Moon	Some Perfect Things	Completing

FIGURE 12: THE SENSES OF THE SOUL

From Figure 12, above, arranged by pairs of opposite-complement trigrams:

Trigram	Urimage	Sense
Sun	Some Make Things	Generating
Moon	Some Perfect Things	Completing

Trigram	Urimage	Sense
Lake	Some Are Pulled To Things	Attracting
Mountain	Some Stand Apart From Things	Distancing

Trigram	Urimage	Sense
Fire	Some Find Things	Showing
Water	Some Veil Things	Hiding

Trigram	Urimage	Sense
Lightning	Some Move Things	Surprising
Wind	Some Move Through Things	Adapting

This inventory of the trigrams' urimages and senses presents another portion of the full spectrum of associations making up the ancestral memory of the archetypes. The urimages detailed here are relevant to the archetypal activities within the dream space. Just as it is naive to think of oneself as the only real being in the world surrounded by dead matter, it is naive to think of oneself as the only real being in the dream space surrounded by dead images. Just as the world itself is the living body of the World Soul, the dream space is the living body of the One Mind. All that one encounters in the dream space is alive, each image the embodiment of an individual Idea of the One Mind. *All* within the dream space is a living image, a symbol of an individual Idea of the One Mind. In consequence, one entering the dream space is, oneself, a living symbol of an individual Idea of the One Mind and perceived as such by all that one encounters.

Mapping Figure 12 onto the Inner Compass produces a second, synonymous, version:

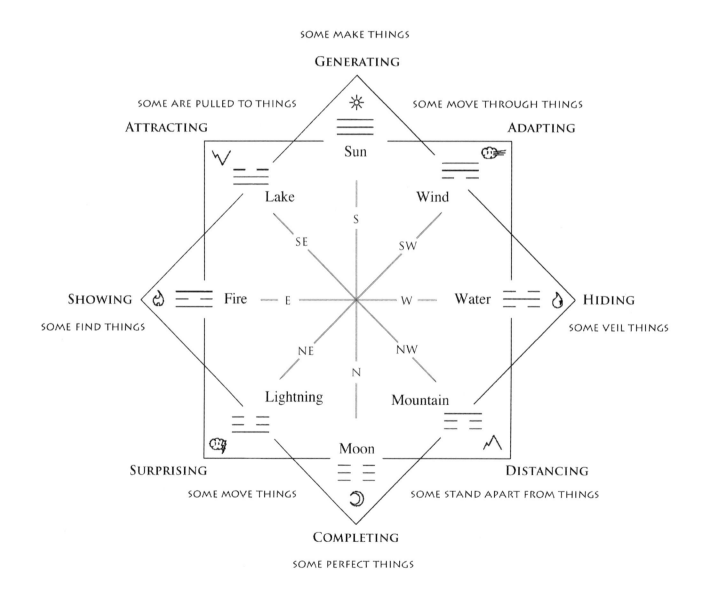

FIGURE 13: INNER COMPASS II

Wherever one stands in the dream space, one stands in the center of the Inner Compass, surrounded by the eight archetypal regions of *formative substance*. To move from the center to one of the eight regions, it is necessary to change one's inner state—an act made possible by *consciously taking on the attribute of the region* in question. To move to the SUN region, in other words, one changes one's internal state to one of *generating*, identifying with that place where *some make things*. Similarly, to move to the LIGHTNING region, one changes one's inner state to one of *surprising*, identifying with that place where *some move things*.

In this sense, "changing inner state" means *consciously identifying with a trigram's attribute*. Because one enters the dream space with a particular inner state, it is necessary to bring it to neutral equipoise, a balanced state reflective of the Before Heaven arrangement itself. This is especially important, as practitioners are often entering the dream space in order to perform some function, often to aid someone in distress or crisis. For this reason, it is often necessary to calm one's internal state, authentically returning to the center before performing one's work. The center of the inner compass is its own particular region, then—one identified with the benevolent awareness of the timeless soul.

It can be good practice to recognize one's inner state during everyday activities in the world of the five senses and develop the discipline to change it consciously. Most people are not aware of their inner state as something that has become habituated and is open to conversion.[16] They are thus surprised to realize that they have spent a large portion of their time in a trancelike state of anxiety or frustration or helplessness or resentment—and even more surprised to realize there are ways to break that trance and transform their inner state to more life-affirming ones. Acquiring the skills to consciously change the personality's internal state within the world of the five senses reinforces the soul's capacity to change its internal state within the dream space—and vice versa.

When first adapting to the dream space, it is best to return to the center of the inner compass before moving from one region to another. Coming back to center, clearing one's intentions—this generally makes for the smoothest transitions from region to region. With experience, however, practitioners find it increasingly straightforward to move directly between regions.

---

[16] See my *The Five Emanations: Aligning the Modern Mind with the Ancient Soul* and *The Spiritual Basis of Good Fortune: Retracing the Ancient Path of Personal Transformation*

THE SHIFT

Shift to the region where some make things
Shift to the region where some are pulled to things
Shift to the region where some find things
Shift to the region where some move things
Shift to the region where some move through things
Shift to the region where some veil things
Shift to the region where some stand apart from things
Shift to the region where some perfect things

What is it that shifts? That with which one identifies.

"Let me see your bowl of stew," Master Khigh Alx Dhiegh would tell me, motioning for me to cup my hands into a bowl. He would make a show of looking into my "bowl" and naming each of the ingredients he saw there. "Carrot. Celery. Onion. Potato." And so on, until he would suddenly instruct me to turn the bowl upside-down. He would take my hands in his and shake them vigorously, "emptying out the bowl" and, once satisfied, pull a handkerchief from a pocket and fastidiously wipe out the inside of the "bowl." At last, beaming like the Laughing Buddha himself, he would hand me back my hands and announce, "There! Now you have a clean bowl!" What is "in my mind" is not *my mind*. I could identify with the stew of experiences that occupied my mind *or* I could identify with the intrinsically clear mind that held them. *What was I?* my teacher was demanding of me—*the bowl or its contents?*

One's identity literally depends on what one identifies with. Feelings of not being worthy enough, for example—feelings nearly all souls entertain in the face of the immensity of Creation. The *shift*, then, begins by shifting what one is paying attention to (as in an earlier example of shifting attention to actively listening to a song that had been in the background of attention). In this example, shifting one's attention from feelings of not being worthy enough to the attributes of, let us say, the trigram MOON. The next phase of the *shift* is to stop identifying with one's habitual sense of self and fully identify with a region's attributes, especially its urimage: *Some perfect things*. This *shift* of identification converts (continuing the present example) "Some perfect things" into *I join those perfecting things*. Joining other souls in the shared activity of their region allows one to align one's intent with theirs by virtue of the momentum that has been building across ages.

This third phase of the *shift* entails entering these regions, making it possible for one to participate in their respective activities—*making things, being pulled to things, finding things, moving things, moving through things, veiling things, standing apart from things, perfecting things*. Such are the archetypal activities of the community of souls within the dream space—activities that marshal the pre-manifestation *formative substance* into inevitable manifestation. One aligns one's individual intent with the collective intent of the region by generating images based on the attributes of its archetype. One uses the momentum of the ancestral archetype, in other words, to carry one's intentional image into the *formative substance* and reinforce its emergence into manifestation. No list of archetype attributes is ever complete—they are catalogs of related concepts and images that practitioners first memorize and learn to recognize underpinning appearances and then, secondly, begin building up the list of attributes by adding their own related concepts and images based on first-hand experience.

By way of an example, let us say that there are changes in one's workplace and new management makes the work environment a starkly unpleasant place to be, casting doubt on the benefit of continuing to work there. First, one might look as clearly as possible at the situation, finding the negative archetype at play. Is it SUN, a new poorly-conceived beginning? Probably not the joy of LAKE, unless it is causing people to unite against the changes. FIRE, with its emphasis on rationality and possible blindness to emotional needs? Perhaps LIGHTNING, an unpleasant shock? Or WIND, a discontent permeating every level of the workplace? Certainly, it could be WATER, with its sense of uncertainty and risk. Or MOUNTAIN, as well, with its disruption and isolation. Or is it MOON in the sense of the end of a beneficial cycle? Identifying the trigram can only be done by applying the attributes to the situation at hand—and doing so *by feel* rather than conceptualization. One must determine the archetype of the situation by its resonance with one's soul sense.

To continue with the example, one might next look to the Inner Compass in order to determine the region of *formative substance* from which to respond to the matter at hand. Is it SUN, an inventive strategy to initiate a new well-conceived beginning? Perhaps LAKE, with its power to draw people together in mutually beneficial collaborations. Or FIRE, with its emphasis on bringing matters to light? Perhaps LIGHTNING, as a surprise maneuver? Or WIND, a gradual and patient strategy of attrition?

Certainly, it could be WATER, with its sense of successfully cloaking one's intentions. Or MOUNTAIN, as well, as withdrawal and a parting of the ways. Or is it MOON in the sense of the end of a destructive cycle? All these are extensions of the attributes of the archetypes' urimages—*making things, being pulled to things, finding things, moving things, moving through things, veiling things, standing apart from things, perfecting things*. Again, it has to be stressed that this must be done by feel—there is no way to construct hypothetical examples that register at the soul level of experience nor any way to conceptualize what is essentially a non-conceptual experience.

With that said, to complete the example, one enters the region that resonates with the soul's response to the matter at hand: *I join those who make things*. Using the attributes of SUN, one fashions an image of a positive, benevolent new beginning: light-giving, magnanimous as sunlight shining for all, dawning with a promise of advancement and adventure, a new era of opportunity for all concerned. Investing the image with one's pure intention, absent any ulterior motive, one entrusts one's image to the living current of the *formative substance*. It is the vision of the archetype and its attributes that is the subject of one's concentration and not the manner or time in which it is achieved. Light from a distant star takes many years to reach one's eyes, yet no sooner than it sets out across space is its arrival already assured—acting in full faith of the *formative substance's* capacity to manifest change, one aligns one's intent to those of all beings *making things*.

SUMMARY

Familiarize yourself with the trigrams and their attributes.

Recognize that they mirror the fundamental reality as well as your own soul's senses.

Sensitize yourself to the formative substance translating reality into appearances.

Learn to perceive the eight archetypal regions of the dream space of the Imaginal.

Identify with the collective activity of each region.

Participate in the collective activity of each region.

Radiate images that channel the formative substance into beneficial manifestation.

2. REALITY

On a moonless, starless night, a single lightningbolt falls, illuminating the entire world for an instant. But in that instant, one sees it all, a sight emblazoned upon one's memory forever, so that no matter how much time passes, that vision of the whole remains ever bright.

"No one can ever know everything," Master Khigh Alx Dhiegh was fond of telling me. "But anyone can understand everything."

What one glimpses in that instant of illumination is not all the things in the world—it is the *relationships between all things* that bursts through the darkness.

To know everything would be to know all the things in the world.

To understand everything is to know the relationships between all the things in the world.

And, as my teacher taught, this understanding is something that anyone can achieve.

Contrary to appearances, the world is not made up of things.

It is made up of relationships between things.

This is meant neither abstractly nor metaphorically. Even the physical sun is not a "thing" but the relationship between things: pressure and temperature give rise to nuclear fusion as protons are merged together into atoms of helium under the force of gravity. It is imperative to reach the point of *understanding* and not simply proceed by what we have been taught to *know*. The "things" in the world of the five senses are illusions, the results of hidden relationships between imperceptible elements. The age-old metaphor is that of the waterfall: what we "see" from a distance is the continuous pouring of the cascade and not the individual drops of water of which it is made.

The trigrams do not represent static, fixed things.

The trigrams represent the fluid and changing relationships between things.

This is not entirely unexpected in light of the relativity of *yin* and *yang* depicted in Figure 1 of the Introduction. From this perspective, the trigrams are not "states" or "events" in and of themselves but, rather, transitions or bridges or unions among less perceptible elements—imperceptible to the five senses, they are the archetypal relationships giving form to the infinitely diverse manifestations.

CREATION is the relationship of elements starting something new; an unexplored or unmanifested relationship among elements that initiates a new phase or endeavor.

WONDER is the relationship of elements stirring excitement, enthusiasm and euphoria; an unexplored or unmanifested relationship among elements that produces closer collaboration or communion.

KNOWLEDGE is the relationship of elements forming an individual's personal worldview; an unexplored or unmanifested relationship among elements that synthesizes precedents and past experience into a group's worldview.

MOTIVATION is the relationship of elements inciting sudden change; an unexplored or unmanifested relationship among elements that adds to the momentum of breaking through inertia.

ADAPTATION is the relationship of elements gradually changing along with change; an unexplored or unmanifested relationship among elements that persistently and patiently penetrates every impasse.

MYSTERY is the relationship of elements obscuring activity from sight; an unexplored or unmanifested relationship among elements that masks activities in uncertainty and unpredictability.

INCUBATION is the relationship of elements holding activity in abeyance, providing time to develop; an unexplored or unmanifested relationship among elements that interrupt advance in order to consolidate and prepare for the next development.

COMPLETION is the relationship of elements bringing a cycle to an end; an unexplored or unmanifested relationship among elements that nurtures and ripens the seed of potential.

These straightforward descriptions of the trigrams' archetypal relationships are their *exoteric formulas*. Their *esoteric formulas* are based on the *order of completeness*, especially as depicted in the Before Heaven arrangement of trigrams.

CREATION	WONDER	KNOWLEDGE	MOTIVATION	ADAPTATION	MYSTERY	INCUBATION	COMPLETION
▬▬	▬ ▬	▬▬	▬ ▬	▬▬	▬ ▬	▬▬	▬ ▬
▬▬	▬▬	▬ ▬	▬ ▬	▬▬	▬▬	▬ ▬	▬ ▬
▬▬	▬▬	▬▬	▬▬	▬ ▬	▬ ▬	▬ ▬	▬ ▬

The esoteric formulas treat each of the trigrams as *the relationship between the trigrams before and after it in the order of completeness*. In this sense, they are thought of as the *child* of the preceding and succeeding trigrams. (Example: LAKE stands between SUN and FIRE)

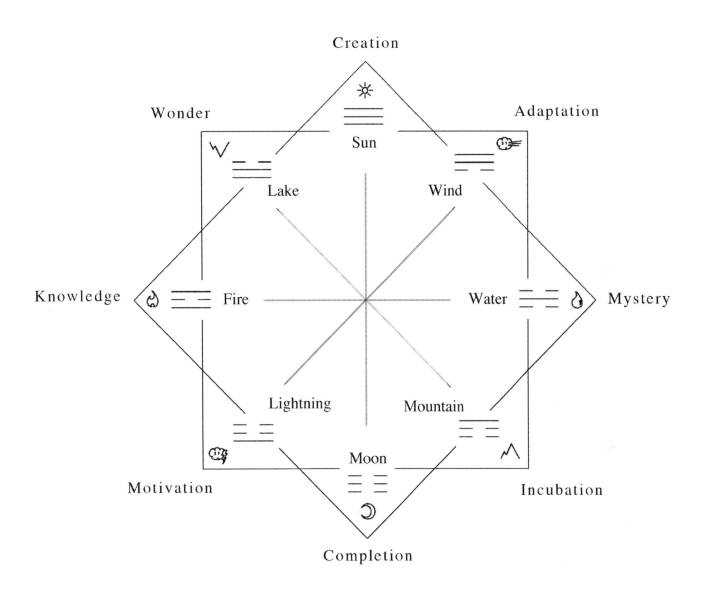

ESOTERIC FORMULAS

SUN is the child of MOON and LAKE

LAKE is the child of SUN and FIRE

FIRE is the child of LAKE and LIGHTNING

LIGHTNING is the child of FIRE and WIND

WIND is the child of LIGHTNING and WATER

WATER is the child of WIND and MOUNTAIN

MOUNTAIN is the child of WATER and MOON

MOON is the child of MOUNTAIN and SUN

Four of these relationships are readily apparent:

> LAKE stands in between SUN and FIRE.
>
> FIRE stands in between LAKE and LIGHTNING.
>
> WATER stands in between WIND and MOUNTAIN.
>
> MOUNTAIN stands in between WATER and MOON.

The other four relationships are less readily apparent due to the peculiarities of mapping the *order of completeness* onto the Before Heaven arrangement. Specifically, they are caused by the order crossing the vertical axis between SUN and MOON and the diagonal axis between LIGHTNING and WIND. Consequently, SUN, LIGHTNING, WIND and MOON are all either preceded or succeeded by a trigram across their respective axis:

> SUN stands in between MOON and LAKE.
>
> LIGHTNING stands in between FIRE and WIND.
>
> WIND stands in between LIGHTNING and WATER.
>
> MOON stands in between MOUNTAIN and SUN.

The esoteric formulas are expanded by augmenting them with their archetypal attributes, providing a fuller reading of the Imaginal elements perceptible only to the soul—

CREATION is the relationship between COMPLETION and WONDER: it is the ORIGIN that blossoms when CONSUMMATION encounters COMMUNION—the INITIATION that carries the FULFILLMENT OF PURPOSE into the ECSTATIC LIFE.

WONDER is the relationship of elements between CREATION and KNOWLEDGE: it is the AWE that blossoms when the ACT OF CREATION encounters SELF-AWARENESS—the EXCITEMENT AND ANTICIPATION that accompanies NEW UNDERTAKINGS and NEW REALIZATIONS.

KNOWLEDGE is the relationship between WONDER and MOTIVATION: it is the LEARNING that blossoms when CURIOSITY encounters SURPRISE—the thirst for NEW KNOWLEDGE that is reawakened when one's ASPIRATIONS take an UNEXPECTED TURN.

MOTIVATION is the relationship between KNOWLEDGE and ADAPTATION: it is the BREAKTHROUGH OF INERTIA that blossoms when EXISTING KNOWLEDGE encounters UNAVOIDABLE ADAPTATION—the PROVOCATION TO CHANGE when PAST EXPERIENCE proves out of step with CHANGING CIRCUMSTANCES.

ADAPTATION is the relationship between MOTIVATION and MYSTERY: it is the EVOLUTION that blossoms when THE UNEXPECTED encounters THE UNKNOWN—the GRADUAL ASSIMILATION that reconciles SHOCK and RISK.

MYSTERY is the relationship between ADAPTATION and INCUBATION: it is the UNCERTAINTY that blossoms when an IRRESISTIBLE FORCE encounters an IMMOVABLE OBJECT—the UNPREDICTABILITY that arises when ENDURING DETERMINATION meets ENDURING RESISTANCE.

INCUBATION is the relationship between MYSTERY and COMPLETION: it is the GESTATION that blossoms when THE UNKNOWN encounters DESTINY—the STILLPOINT that tempers the RIDDLE OF LIFE with the REALIZATION OF POTENTIAL.

COMPLETION is the relationship between INCUBATION and CREATION: it is the INEVITABLE that blossoms when GESTATION encounters BIRTH—the END OF A CYCLE that arrives when INNER DEVELOPMENT gives way to a NEW GENERATION.

These formulas are all keys used to *break through space* and gain entry into their corresponding regions. The regions themselves are visualized slightly differently, however.

This difference is demonstrated in Figure 14, below, which is based on the structural *octants* of the Before Heaven arrangement rather than the *order of completeness*.

The *octants* focus on the eight divisions of the Before Heaven arrangement, each depicting one of the regions. The octants are named for their respective compass directions and include the regions to either side.

By way of example, the octant of SUN is named SOUTH and includes the regions to either side, WIND and LAKE. In Figure 14, the regions are referred to by their archetypal attributes (to continue the example: CREATION stands in between ADAPTATION and WONDER)—

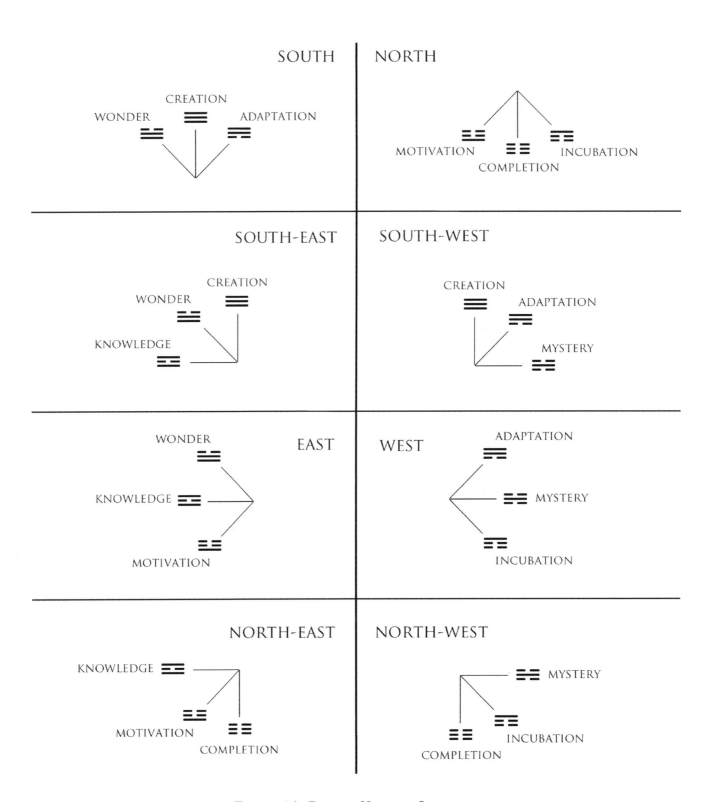

FIGURE 14: BEFORE HEAVEN OCTANTS

The regions are visualized as octants because of their shared boundaries, an indication that the dream space of the *Imaginal* is not ordered by divisions of exclusivity but, rather, by relationships of proximity. The tripartite nature of each region does not mean that each octant does not possess its own distinctive character but it does mean that the dream space of the *Imaginal* is profoundly altered by a change in the arrangement of the trigrams. The octant FIRE surrounded by LAKE and LIGHTNING, in other words, has a wholly different character than one in which FIRE is surrounded by WIND and MOON.[17]

The evolution of the manner in which the dream space of the *Imaginal* is visualized—from a focus on the compass directions to a focus on the octants—opens the gateway to a fuller participation in the archetypal regions of reality underlying the diverse manifestations of appearances.

From Compass To Map

When your stand and reality are one, your intent and manifestation are one

The Inner Compass provides the soul a way to orient itself within the dream space of the *Imaginal*. By internalizing the Inner Compass—and especially its archetypal attributes—one can identify the direction and momentum of the pre-manifestation *formative substance* at work imperceptible to the five senses. When it comes to entering the regions, though, it is useful to have *reflections* of the *Imaginal* in mind—

SUN: *A bright field of wildflowers, the sun just rising on the distant horizon*

LAKE: *A large lake ringed by plants and trees, the water and sky host to flocks of birds*

FIRE: *Atop a distant cliff, a signal fire beckons beneath the glistening stars*

LIGHTNING: *On a moonless, starless night, a single lightningbolt illuminates the world*

WIND: *A tree on a hill in a field, its autumn leaves flying away in the wind*

WATER: *A spectacular waterfall cascading into a deep chasm, mist rising on updrafts*

MOUNTAIN: *A great mountain rising out of the plains, its summit ringed in clouds*

MOON: *From a silvery shore, the four phases of the moon hovering above the sea*

---

[17] As in the After Heaven (Houtian) arrangement, which is closer to the world of manifestation than the Before Heaven (Xiantian) arrangement. See my *Image and Number Treatise*.

It is in this way that the Before Heaven arrangement metamorphoses from a compass into a map.

Figure 15, below, shows how the compass directions have opened up into their respective regions based on the interstitial space of the octants—

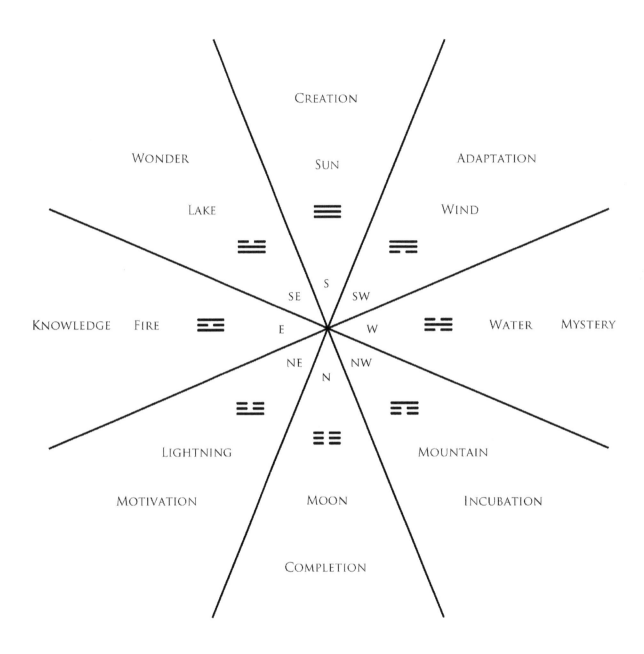

FIGURE 15: MAP OF EIGHT REGIONS

From this perspective, the *reflections* of the *Imaginal* "fill in" their respective octants, investing them with a living *presence*. Practitioners taking up a stance at the center point of this map find themselves turning in a circle, gazing into each of the eight *landscapes*, or *reflections*, in turn. The regions thus lose any semblance of abstraction, transmuted by the esoteric formulas into spiritual landscapes as tangible to the soul as the physical universe is to the body.

In no sense are these descriptions of the *reflections* intended to be comprehensive. They are simply the archetypal views from the center of the dream space. Once one enters the *Imaginal*, the landscape of the regions open up onto wider and further vistas, each region an infinitude of living images and soul experiences.

Without the compass and map, however, entry into the dream space appears chaotic and random, an ever-changing landscape of beings whose relationships confound the soul's senses.[18] This is not just a concern of the living practitioner, though, since it is here, too, that the soul dwells after death provided it has established a footing. Without first-hand experience of the dream space, the soul risks wandering among unsettling, chaotic and random images, reliving the memories of its deceased body and mistaking those memories for life in the world of the five senses.[19]

Within each region one finds groups of souls who have taken refuge—some still in body, some long discarnate. These communities provide one with allies, collaborators and teachers.[20] Collective endeavors are the norm here rather than the exception—still, one must ever be mindful that the dream space is filled with many different souls and that intentions can create backlashes.[21] Whether one works to build in the *Imaginal* or produce effects in the world of manifestation, it is always best to focus one's intent on *Benefiting All At The Same Time*.

The world of appearances mirrors this map as well, of course, for it reveals the structure and function of the *formative substance* in its pre-manifestation state. Orienting oneself to the underlying reality beneath the surface of appearances does not imply a withdrawal from the world of the five senses—on the contrary, it signals a higher degree of participation in life. Those who understand the essence behind

---

[18] Different traditions utilize various schema to help orient the soul. The Pure Land of Buddhism; esoteric Sufism (alam al-mithal, Mundus Imaginalis); the after death landscape of the ancient Mesoamericans; and so on.

[19] I have written about the two soul philosophy and the after-death experience several times—most recently, in my *Way of the Diviner* and, earlier, in my recounting of my own death experience in *The Five Emanations*.

[20] See my *In The Oneness Of Time: The Education Of A Diviner*.

[21] See my *Way of the Diviner*.

existence, after all, have greater resources at their disposal—and greater capacity to marshal those resources toward the common good: this is simply the definition of *wisdom*. If philosophy—and by *philosophy* is literally meant *love of wisdom*—is to have relevance to people's lives, then philosophers, as seers of the underlying reality, must empathize with the state of the poorest among us and choose to remedy the ills of humankind through a sincere dedication to the wellbeing of all.

The body dwells in the world of appearances and it is in the world of appearances that people's wellbeing is manifested. The full potential of humanity cannot be realized so long as generations of groups of people are trapped in poverty, living out entire lifetimes without the basics of adequate shelter, food, water and medical care. So simple a fact is not lost on anyone, yet the world goes on without ever solving such a basic problem. Likewise, the full potential of humanity cannot be realized until people everywhere are collaborating to build a civilization that embodies the *one race of humankind* at peace with itself and nature. Again, so simple a fact and yet—nothing but obstacles millennium after millennium. Why?

Because not every soul in the *Imaginal* is yet filled with light and benevolence.

Fear drives some souls toward greed and hostility, an insatiable need to control their surroundings regardless of the pain or harm it inflicts. These troubled souls—for that is their state until they free themselves of their chains—are repulsed by souls of light-hearted buoyancy and love of Creation. They are drawn together, though, with other troubled souls. Banded together in spiritual fortresses of dark fear and unquenchable greed, their collective intent poisons the *formative substance*: violence, disease, poverty and subjugation of human beings and our living environment—such are the manifestations of the troubled souls' intent. It maintains its pre-manifestation influence on the world of appearances first, by dint of its intensity and, second, by dint of the momentum it has built up over time. And, as people have discovered time after time, the hold these troubled souls have is not easily broken when addressed directly in the world of the five senses—and even when their hold *is* broken, it rises from the ashes and reasserts its dominance anew.

The antidote to this dreadful situation lies in addressing its cause at the root—which means marshaling the collective intent of benevolent souls within the *Imaginal*, helping shape the *formative substance* into manifestations of universal goodwill and magnanimous cooperation. Again, far from implying a retreat from the world of the five senses, such an antidote proves effective only when practitioners remain vigilant to incipient changes in the field of manifestation and help midwife them into full realization. Inspired not by the injustices done to oneself but, rather, by the injustices done to others, practitioners seek the age-old dream of the ancients for a world governed by humaneness and justice. Within the dream space of the *Imaginal*, practitioners find themselves attracted to certain communities of souls and repelled by other communities of souls. An esoteric manifestation of the ancient principle, *Like attracts like*, this attraction is caused by an emotional resonance whereby *essence recognizes essence*: the first-hand experience of such recognition is awash in an aura of homecoming, of finding one's spiritual ancestors.

TALISMANS

There is a threshold between the world of the five senses and the dream space of the *Imaginal*. It is the threshold that the *formative substance* crosses as it emerges into manifestation. Though it has many names, among the most telling is its most ancient name: *The Gate of Coming and Going*. It is here, at this threshold, that practitioners stand watch for the incipient manifestations of *formative substance* in order to detect the direction and momentum of coming change. For this reason, it is also known by its equally ancient name, *The Gate of Divination*.

Herein lies, at first blush, the most readily accessible answer to the question, *Why study the I Ching?* For, as mentioned already, most people associate the I Ching with divination, thinking it a form of ancient fortune-telling. This is an understandable misconception, the result of the body's five senses trying to make sense of what the soul's eight senses perceive. If we step back for a moment and observe the act of the water diviner, then we see that the dowser is not finding *future* water but, rather, *present* water hidden beneath the surface of the ground. Such is the activity of I Ching diviners, as well, who are not detecting future manifestations but present ones hidden beneath the surface of appearances. It is true, nonetheless, that one underground water is merely a trickle and another a formidable river—likewise, some incipient changes are barely discernable and others, powerful currents of coming manifestation. In the latter instance, the strength of the current is such that the direction and momentum of change make it possible to anticipate the development of manifestation with accuracy. Diviners function in that case as a kind of spiritual weathervane, assisting the community with a vision of what is coming through the Gate and what is going back out the Gate.

The deeper function of the diviner, however, falls along more shamanic lines.[22] As practitioners able to enter the dream space of the *Imaginal* and work with the archetypal regions of *formative substance*, diviners benefit the community by *delaying as long as possible the change from times of good fortune* while *hastening as much as possible the change from times of misfortune*. This *delaying-and-hastening* activity requires one to straddle the threshold of coming and going, with one foot in each world in order to track changes in the world of the five senses all the while marshaling the archetypal *formative substance* in the *Imaginal*.

The principle tool in I Ching divination is its 64 hexagrams.[23] Hexagrams are made up of two trigrams, an upper trigram and a lower trigram, as depicted in Figure 8, above. It is all the possible combinations of the eight trigrams that comprise the whole of the 64 hexagrams. The lower trigram is traditionally thought of as the *inner trigram* and the upper trigram as the *outer trigram*. This combination of *inner and outer* images is what allows the hexagrams to be applied to a wide range of situations. For instance, in the case of an individual, the inner symbolizes the person's internal experience, while the outer symbolizes the person's external circumstances. Similarly, in the case of a nation, the inner symbolizes the country's domestic relations, while the outer symbolizes the country's international relations. Since the trigrams themselves are the archetypal elements of experience, the combinations of inner and outer provide for the widest range of correlations to the universe of experience.

The act of divining is a shamanic act because one is seeking help from the spirit world. Whether that help is in the form of better understanding the hidden or clarifying complex decisions, diviners address the spirit world and receive an answer from the spirit world. By its very nature, this is a sacred duty, a sacred trust, especially when performed for other people. It is to be conducted with reverence and an air of solemnity. Neither personal opinion nor specialized knowledge have any place in the repertoire of a diviner's interpretation of the Oracle's response. To be a diviner is to cultivate and exercise the utmost self-discipline of thought and intent, setting aside the personality's experiences in order to allow the soul to convey with unimpeded clarity the Oracle's thought and intent.

---

[22] As discussed in my *In The Oneness Of Time*, spirit-mediums and diviners were the first shamans.
[23] The technique by which to consult the Oracle, either by yarrow stalks or coins, can be found in numerous places online. Since the present work is part of my *Researches on the Toltec I Ching*, it should come as no surprise that I refer the reader to *The Toltec I Ching*—there is a detailed description of the coin method of consulting the Oracle in its Introduction.

The deeper function of the diviner, however, falls to practitioners who are actively entering the spirit world of the *Imaginal* and working with the *formative substance* as part of their *delaying-and-hastening* activity. Such activity is directly related to the use of *talismans* in their role of attracting good fortune and warding off misfortune.

Talismans are spiritually-charged images inscribed during a sacred ritual. Etymologically, the word traces back to Greek *teleō*, meaning *I complete, or perform, a rite*. The use of talismans extends back into the far reaches of antiquity and across every culture. In their role of attracting good fortune and warding off misfortune, their use has traditionally extended into the realms of medicinal cures and help conceiving a child. There are examples, too, of certain costumes, buildings and even individuals themselves being considered talismans. The word likewise traces to a later Greek word, *telein*, meaning *to initiate into the mysteries*, a direct reference to its roots in the esoteric teachings of the mystery schools. From all this, it can be said that talismans are invested with what might be called *inner charisma*.[24] The distinction between talismans, then, and the wider array of magically-charged objects can become blurred by extending the use of the word into the fuller reach of good luck charms, amulets, gemstones, and so on.

In the context of the present work, we confine ourselves to the stricter sense of talismans as *spiritually-charged images inscribed during a sacred ritual*.

- The *images* to be inscribed are the Hexagrams of the I Ching
- The act of *inscribing* refers to writing on paper or parchment or inscribing in clay, etc
- The *sacred ritual* is the act of divination and consulting the Oracle
- The *spiritual charge* of the Hexagram results from the practitioner entering the *Imaginal* with a question and returning with the Hexagram

The hexagrams are spiritually-charged images which, when inscribed during the divinatory ritual with the right intent, are powerful talismans capable of attracting good fortune and warding off misfortune. They are living symbols of psyche, of the soul, that empower the practitioner to address *illnesses* in the manifestation realm by administering *medicines* in the *Imaginal* realm. Hexagrams, in other words, are magical talismans empowering the practitioner's *delaying-and-hastening* activity.

---

[24] See my *The Five Emanations*

Hexagram Talismans

#1 Provoking Change: Lightning / Lightning *Attracts*: Daring Initiative. Overturning Stagnation. *Wards Off*: Discouragement. Procrastination. Resignation.	*#2 Sensing Creation:* Lake / Lake *Attracts*: Nature Mysticism. Immersion in Emotional Lushness of the Spirit of Nature. Forgiveness. *Wards Off*: Encapsulation. Walling Off. Numbing.
#3 Recognizing Ancestry: Wind / Sun *Attracts*: Spiritual Ancestors. Spiritual Homecoming. *Wards Off*: Rootlessness. Homelessness. Lack of Lineage.	*#4 Mirroring Wisdom:* Fire / Wind *Attracts*: Spiritual Teachers. Symbolic Thinking. *Wards Off*: Materialistic Worldview. Self-Interest.
#5 Restoring Wholeness: Wind / Lightning *Attracts*: Healing. Return to Wellbeing. *Wards Off*: Scarring. Infection. Relapse.	*#6 Fostering Self-Sacrifice:* Lightning / Wind *Attracts*: Patience. Others Needing Help. *Wards Off*: Impatience. Bad Judgment.
#7 Compelling Motive: Lake / Wind *Attracts*: Impetuosity. Spontaneity. Self-Assurance. *Wards Off*: Need for Approval. Self-Doubt.	*#8 Harmonizing Duality:* Wind / Lake *Attracts*: Balanced Relationship. Love. *Wards Off*: Dominance. Discord. Misunderstanding.
#9 Uprooting Fear: Water / Lightning *Attracts*: Spiritual Protection. Confidence. Courage. *Wards Off*: Timidity. Insecurity.	*#10 Unifying Inspiration:* Lightning / Moon *Attracts*: Meaningful Work. Collaborative Venture. *Wards Off*: Incompatible Allies. Widespread Discord.
#11 Attracting Allies: Lake / Lightning *Attracts*: Helping Spirits. Unforeseen Aid. *Wards Off*: Aloneness. Hopelessness.	*#12 Seeing Ahead:* Lightning / Lake *Attracts*: Foresight. Planning. Decision-Making. *Wards Off*: Confusion. Indecision.
#13 Concentrating Attention: Lightning / Mountain *Attracts*: Presence of Mind. Lucid Awareness. *Wards Off*: Inattention. Scattered Focus.	*#14 Unlocking Evolution:* Mountain / Lightning *Attracts*: Metamorphosis. Collective Transformation. *Wards Off*: Stagnation. Habit Mind. Triviality.
#15 Belonging Together: Lake / Fire *Attracts*: Intimacy. Emotional Bonding. *Wards Off*: Isolation. Homesickness. Grief.	*#16 Renewing Devotion:* Sun / Lake *Attracts*: Discovering Deeper Meaning to Purpose. *Wards Off*: Second Thoughts. Ambivalence.
#17 Guiding Force: Moon / Sun *Attracts*: Spirit Guide. Spiritual Twin. *Wards Off*: Fear of the Unknown. Spiritual Paralysis.	*#18 Resolving Paradox:* Fire / Water *Attracts*: Win-Win Solution. *Wards Off*: Thinking In Polarities.

#19 Celebrating Passage: Lake / Moon *Attracts*: Sharing Life's Joys and Sorrows. *Wards Off*: Melancholy. Downheartedness.	*#20 Entering Service: Water / Lake* *Attracts*: Magnanimous Intent. *Wards Off*: Lack of Compassion. Biases.
#21 Cultivating Character: Mountain / Sun *Attracts*: Preparing for Next Stage. Independence. *Wards Off*: Self-Satisfaction. Vanity.	*#22 Sharing Memory: Fire / Mountain* *Attracts*: Self-Remembering. Akashic Record. *Wards Off*: Soul's Amnesia.
#23 Wielding Passion: Fire / Lake *Attracts*: Life-Affirming Endeavors. Whole-Hearted Adventurousness. *Wards Off*: Emotional Repression. Faint-Heartedness.	*#24 Revealing Knowledge: Lake / Sun* *Attracts*: Discovery. Revelation. *Wards Off*: Preconceptions. Opinions. Jumping to Conclusions.
#25 Radiating Intent: Lightning / Sun *Attracts*: Noble-Minded Organization. *Wards Off*: Misleading Allies. Betrayal of Trust.	*#26 Dignifying Ambition: Fire / Lightning* *Attracts*: Benevolent Striving. Worthy Purpose. *Wards Off*: Conflict. Competition.
#27 Trusting Intuition: Fire / Sun *Attracts*: Clear-Sighted Presentiment. Sensitivity to Incipient Change. *Wards Off*: Negative Imagination. Undue Influence.	*#28 Synchronizing Movement: Moon / Water* *Attracts*: Timing. Fittingness. Magically-Right Moment. Kairos. *Wards Off*: Mistiming. Missed Opportunities.
#29 Sustaining Resilience: Wind / Wind *Attracts*: Flexibility. Accommodation. Bending. Tempered. Non-resistance. Frictionless. *Wards Off*: Breaking. Stubborn Fixity. Need to be Right. Self-Righteousness.	*#30 Transforming Extinction: Mountain / Mountain* *Attracts*: Revering Mortality. Remembering Lifetimes. Transcending Birth and Death. *Wards Off*: Despair. Dread. Fear and Repression of Mortality.
#31 Embracing Noninterference: Moon / Fire *Attracts*: Wise Interaction. Enlightened Relationships. Compassionate Nonintervention. *Wards Off*: Undue Influence. Intimidation. Seduction.	*#32 Controlling Confrontation: Sun / Water* *Attracts*: Reasoned Discourse. Self-Control. Compromise. Amnesty. *Wards Off*: Conflict. Aggression. Antagonism. Projection.
#33 Accepting Instruction: Lightning / Fire *Attracts*: Strength to Withstand Pressures of Social Convention. Free-Thinking. Spiritual Teachings. *Wards Off*: Cultural Blindness. Social Prejudices. Fanaticism.	*#34 Evoking Opposite: Sun / Lightning* *Attracts*: Spiritual Protectors. Invisibility. *Wards Off*: Hostile Intentions. Being taken Advantage of. Personality Conflicts.

#35 Holding Back: Mountain / Lake *Attracts*: Securing the Valuable. *Wards Off*: Thieves. Loss by Trickery or Manipulation. Habitual Reflexes.	*#36 Stabilizing Communion: Lake / Mountain* *Attracts*: Peace. Tranquility. At-One-Ment with Nature and Divine. Continuity of Heart-Mind. *Wards Off*: Distractibility. Discontent. Fault-finding. Criticism.
#37 Penetrating Confusion: Water / Mountain *Attracts*: Ability to See through Illusion. *Wards Off*: Deceivers. Misinformation. Too Easily Influenced.	*#38 Dissolving Artifice: Mountain / Moon* *Attracts*: Will to Authenticity. Opportunity to Search for Greater Meaning. *Wards Off*: Social Conditioning. Pursuit of Status.
#39 Reviving Tradition: Wind / Fire *Attracts*: Wisdom Teachings of the Old Ones. *Wards Off*: Materialism. Desecration of Spirit.	*#40 Adapting Experience: Sun / Wind* *Attracts*: New Response to Changing Conditions. Reconfiguring Resources. Old Skills for New Purpose. *Wards Off*: Over-Reliance on Precedent.
#41 Feigning Compliance: Fire / Moon *Attracts*: Trickster. Outwitting Oppression. *Wards Off*: Dominance. Helplessness. Victimization.	*#42 Interpreting Insight: Water / Sun* *Attracts*: Originality of Self-Expression. New Associations. Courage to Confront Wrong-Doing. *Wards Off*: Authoritarianism. Intimidation.
#43 Going Beyond: Moon / Lightning *Attracts*: Metamorphic Leap. Will to Transcendence. *Wards Off*: Self-Satisfaction. Others' Definition of Human Being.	*#44 Refining Instinct: Lightning / Water* *Attracts*: Self-Discipline. *Wards Off*: Self-Defeating Habits.
#45 Casting Off: Moon / Lake *Attracts*: Unconditional Acceptance of Self and Others. *Wards Off*: Judgmental Attitude. Correcting Others.	*#46 Honoring Contentment: Lake / Water* *Attracts*: Awareness of Perfection of Moment. *Wards Off*: Restlessness. Frustration.
#47 Making Individual: Moon / Wind *Attracts*: Self-Discovery. Authenticity. Freedom via Ordeal. *Wards Off*: Conformity. Social Identity.	*#48 Moving Source: Wind / Water* *Attracts*: Embodying the Unknown Self. Unpredictability. Ongoing Creation. *Wards Off*: Stagnation. Meaningless Work.
#49 Staying Open: Moon / Mountain *Attracts*: Generalization. Abundance of Choices. *Wards Off*: Specialization.	*#50 Narrowing Aim: Mountain / Water* *Attracts*: Focused Aim. Specialization. *Wards Off*: Over-extending Self. Too many Interests.

#51 Living Essence: Sun / Sun *Attracts*: Spirit of the Seed. Living Potential. Untroubled Spirit. *Wards Off*: Troubled Spirit. Superficial Perceptions. Trivial Actions. Trying to Control Consequences.	*#52 Growing Certainty: Fire / Fire* *Attracts*: Living Evolving Truth. *Wards Off*: Dogma. Proselytization. Conformity.
#53 Mastering Reason: Water / Fire *Attracts*: The Great Mystery. The Creative Duality. *Wards Off*: Over-Reliance on Rationality. Desecration of Matter.	*#54 Repeating Test: Sun / Moon* *Attracts*: Healing the Past. Starting Over. Second Chance. *Wards Off*: Repeating Pattern of Self-Defeating Habit.
#55 Internalizing Purity: Sun / Mountain *Attracts*: Perfecting Heart and Face. *Wards Off*: Self-Indulgence.	*#56 Recapturing Vision: Mountain / Fire* *Attracts*: Altruistic Idealism. *Wards Off*: Cynicism. World-Weariness.
#57 Defying Uncertainty: Water / Water *Attracts*: Faith. Trust in Life. Indomitable Spirit. *Wards Off*: Being Overwhelmed. Victimization. Stress.	*#58 Dawning Existence: Moon / Moon* *Attracts*: Prospering. Comfort. Contentment. Nurture. Giving. Kind-Heartedness. Fulfillment. *Wards Off*: Anxiety. Unease. Loss.
#59 Developing Potential: Water / Wind *Attracts*: Unforeseeable Success. Long-Shot. *Wards Off*: Incurious. Being Forgotten. Forgetting.	*#60 Changing Alliances: Wind / Moon* *Attracts*: Continuity in Change. Good Ending. *Wards Off*: Anger. Hurt. Resentment. Jealousy.
#61 Strengthening Integrity: Water / Moon *Attracts*: Mutual Respect and Appreciation. *Wards Off*: Taking for Granted. Familiarity Breeding Contempt.	*#62 Conceiving Spirit: Sun / Fire* *Attracts*: Immortal Spirit Body. *Wards Off*: Leaking Life Force.
#63 Awakening Self-Sufficiency: Wind / Mountain *Attracts*: Freedom In Every Sense. Proactive Adaptation. *Wards Off*: Dependence. Maladaptation.	*#64 Safeguarding Life: Mountain / Wind* *Attracts*: The Universal Civilizing Spirit. *Wards Off*: Blindness to the Desecration of Nature and Human Nature.

FIGURE 16: HEXAGRAM TALISMANS

Figure 16, above, details the hexagrams and their *talismanic efficacies*. It presents each hexagram number and name from *The Toltec I Ching*. It also details the upper and lower trigrams making up each hexagram, so that, for example, *Mountain / Wind* indicates that Mountain is the upper trigram and Wind is the lower. What is *attracted* is a beneficial kind of *formative substance* in the dream space of the *Imaginal*, while what is *warded off* is a detrimental kind of manifestation in the world of the five senses.

Figure 17, below, presents the 64 hexagram-talismans of the I Ching.

FIGURE 17: THE TOLTEC I CHING HEXAGRAM SEQUENCE

Taken together, Figures 16 and 17 comprise a standalone system of *talismanic divination*.

Use of the hexagrams as talismans may proceed in one of two ways, dependent on circumstances.

The first technique is to consult the Oracle in one's typical fashion, either by the yarrow stalk or coin method. The resulting divinatory hexagram[25] is inscribed on the appropriate medium while the diviner-practitioner still journeys in the dream space of the *Imaginal*. Upon returning to the world of the five senses, the diviner identifies the divinatory hexagram via the chart presented in Figure 18, below.[26] The corresponding hexagram number in Figure 16 yields the focus of the *delaying-and-hastening* activity in the form of *attracting and warding off* efficacies.

Locate the hexagram number at the intersection of its upper and lower trigrams:

Upper → / Lower ↓	☰	☱	☲	☳	☴	☵	☶	☷
☰	2	23	8	45	16	12	20	35
☱	15	52	39	31	62	33	53	56
☲	7	4	29	47	40	6	59	64
☳	19	41	60	58	54	10	61	38
☴	24	27	3	17	51	25	42	21
☵	11	26	5	43	34	1	9	14
☶	46	18	48	28	32	44	57	50
☷	36	22	63	49	55	13	37	30

FIGURE 18: THE TOLTEC I CHING HEXAGRAM IDENTIFICATION CHART

Continuing the example above, the divinatory hexagram consisting of upper trigram Mountain and lower trigram Wind is identified as hexagram number 64 in Figure 18. The corresponding hexagram number

---

[25] Ignoring for the act of inscription any changing lines.
[26] The resulting hexagram numbers apply to The Toltec I Ching arrangement. Readers interested in the traditional King Wen arrangement will find a similar chart in the version they are using.

in Figure 16 yields the following talismanic charge: *Attracts: The Universal Civilizing Spirit. Wards Off: Blindness to the Desecration of Nature and Human Nature.*

This first technique yields a talisman in response to a divinatory inquiry—the hexagram is the Oracle's reply to one's question, the reflection from the spirit world of the object of one's investigation. This charges the hexagram with a talismanic potency that *in and of itself possesses efficacy*: it has crossed the threshold of the Gate of Coming and Going and entered the world of manifestation, itself an embodied archetypal image of the *formative substance*. The inscribed hexagram is then worn on the individual's person or made part of an altar or kept on a bed stand. Although it serves well for the practitioner to re-enter the *Imaginal* and take up dwelling in the regions corresponding to the upper and lower trigrams, the essential work has already been accomplished—the talisman has entered into the world of the five senses and, like the light of a distant star that has not yet reached us, the changes it has evoked are already on their way.

The second technique does not involve the act of divination. Instead, the practitioner:

- Identifies the "illness" manifesting in the world of the five senses
- Identifies the corresponding hexagram by its "warding off" efficacy
- Journeys into the dream space of the *Imaginal* holding the hexagram image in mind
- Takes up dwelling in the region corresponding to the hexagram's upper trigram
- Elicits the collective evocation of the hexagram with other beings in that region
- Performs a ritual with those other beings by virtue of planting the talisman in that region
- Inscribes the hexagram onto its medium
- Returns to the world of the five senses with the talisman

One *identifies the corresponding hexagram by its "warding off" efficacy* in the sense that the "illness" one has identified has an archetypal image that envelops it. Continuing the example above, we could say that one recognizes that governmental agencies are failing to protect fragile environments—looking through the inventory of Hexagram Talismans, one comes to hexagram 64, the "wards off" portion of which reads, *Blindness to the Desecration of Nature and Human Nature*. One determines that this reflects the underlying problem perfectly and so settles on hexagram 64, *Safeguarding Life*.

Planting the talisman in the corresponding region refers to the practice of recognizing that the talisman is a living symbol, a seed of intent, that is sown in the ground of the *formative substance*—a seed that takes root, thrives and casts its own seeds into the field of eternity. Performing the seeding ritual with the other beings of that region is an archetypal ceremony that *returns to the Act of Creation* and unfolds without any conscious direction or preconception.

In both methods, the diviner-practitioner is actively working in one realm in order to effect beneficial change in the other. This is the higher-order work to be accomplished at the threshold between the world of the five senses and the dream space of the *Imaginal*. Straddling the threshold in this manner helps uncover a deeper meaning to the question, *Why study the I Ching?* for it is not just perception and reality that are the same—in the primal non-duality, the practitioner and reality are one and the same, mutually influencing one another in the Great Work of bringing the *first ancestors' vision of paradise* to full realization. Such work is not restricted to the world of manifestation, as there remain conclaves of troubled souls still dwelling within the dream space of the *Imaginal*—troubled souls whose self-destructive intentions still bubble out into the world of manifestation.[27]

The esoteric rule of thumb governing their mutually influencing intents is this:

Outer change evokes inner response.
Inner change evokes outer response.

THE DREAM BODY

From the perspective of the body, the soul is the dream body.
From the perspective of the soul, the body is the dream body.

To directly see reality without conceptualization is one thing.
To participate directly in reality without mortality is another.

Direct seeing depends on not relying on the human senses.
Direct participation depends on not relying on the human body.

---

[27] See my *Way of the Diviner.*

To enter into the dream space of the *Imaginal* is to journey in the spirit world. This is a journey that the human body cannot make. The journeying body has many names. The diamond body. The immortal spirit body. The double. The twin. The spirit companion. The higher soul. The *hun*. The *nagual*. The shamanic body. And so on, across cultures and ages.

Because the *Imaginal* consists solely of living images that act much like those in dreams, the space in which it all exists is called *dream space* and the body that participates in it is called the *dream body*. None of which should be interpreted as a lack of substantiality or solidity, as the following formula demonstrates:

The world of the five senses is real but temporary.
The world of the soul is real and permanent.

As everyone's experience with dreams teaches, experiences in the dream state not only feel more real than waking life but more intimate, in the sense of immediacy of emotional impact and meaningfulness. The objective reality of the dream space is what the five senses deny—and what the eight senses affirm:

Reality is where you spend eternity.

Just as it takes an entire physical universe to sustain one's physical body, it takes an entire spiritual universe to sustain one's spirit body. That these two universes are ultimately one is self-evident, as the *prima materia*, the *formative substance*, of the dream space crystalizes and generates the world of manifestation. Also self-evident, however, is the fact that the *laws of physics* governing the world of the five senses are very different than the *laws of psyche* that govern the world of the soul. While the spatiality of the *Imaginal* is objectively real, there is no time there in the way that there is in the world of manifestation—time *is* psyche, an oceanic oneness coincident with omnipresent spirit:

We Are Time.

To say that there is no past, present or future is still deficient, as the rational mind interprets this to say that one ought dwell solely in the present. The ancients address this miscalculation by saying, *Do not even fall into the present*. The reason, of course, is that as soon as one conceptualizes the present, one has conceived the past and future. Relax the mind, stop thinking in terms of time and dwell in a wholly spatial world in which the order of events follows the *law of spiritual cause-and-effect* rather than following the "arrow of time" to which the five senses are accustomed.

The "matter" of the spirit world is composed wholly of images, regardless of whether the image is one of a vast plain, a snowstorm, a mountain range, a clear sky, a night sky of galaxies, an eclipse of sun and moon, a planet seen from above, a wide sea, a raindrop, an atom, a photon, a black hole or nova—all are living images no less vital and aware than the plants, trees, animals and other beings dwelling in the dream space.

> *Just as there is one sun, so too is there one moon.*
> *Just as there is one spirit, so too is there one body.*

Awareness—the vehicle of perception and fount of action—is a microcosm of the macrocosmic *unity-within-duality*. On the individual level, awareness is the binding agent forever suspended between revelation (of the mystery of Creation) and self-revelation (of the mystery of one's own nature), as expressed in this ancient formula:

> *Inside the mind, another mind.*
> *Outside the body, another body.*

This *mind within the mind* is the awakened mind, the intrinsically enlightened mind, of which it is difficult to speak openly.[28] The *body outside the body* is the immortal spirit body, the dream body, which is cultivated through a praxis that sensitizes its practitioners to the hidden reality behind appearances and empowers them to participate in a beneficial way within that hidden reality.

The dream body is also named the *intentional body*. Everything the diviner-practitioner-shaman does is a direct expression of intent. The act of moving within the dream space, which is accomplished by changing internal states, is an intentional act. The act of perceiving the archetypal regions, which is accomplished by honing the eight senses of the soul, is an intentional act. The act of emanating beneficial intent, which is accomplished by eradicating self-interest, is an intentional act. The act of *delaying-and-hastening* changes of fortune, which is accomplished by attracting goodwill and warding off ill will, is an intentional act.

Encountering the communities of souls that have occupied the dream space since time immemorial, the diviner-practitioner-shaman comes to experience the full power of intent. Indigenous peoples have for ages established and sustained enclaves within the regions of the *Imaginal*. Different peoples possessed

---

[28] See my *Way of the Diviner*.

differing reasons and purposes for doing so but certainly one, as global history moved into the period of cultures colonizing other cultures, was (and remains) the "carving out" of a sanctuary for their souls. Their enclaves provided (and continue to provide) a safe haven for them to live the meaningful and sacred lifeway of their ancestors. Even as their bodies toil beneath the strain of ongoing injustice and inhumanity, their souls keep alive a time before the interruption of their culture. Such refuges are the true dwelling places of their people. Among those living in the world of manifestation, they are the home to which people return in ceremonies, celebrations and rituals. Among those living in the spirit world, they are the paradises evoked by the original ancestors. In both cases, it is the collective intent of their people that has established and continues to sustain these homelands for the dream body.

Other types of communities exist within the *Imaginal*, however—in particular, those deriving from some religions and spiritual practices, most notably those able to maintain tradition and ritual. Others are more *ad hoc*, born of shared deep-seated urges within the soul—the influence of such communities ranges from the most beneficial to the most detrimental. Again, it is the collective intent of its inhabitants that provides the stability of such enclaves.

One may journey the eight regions of the spirit world and never encounter such enclaves, for part of their enduring abode is the result of secretiveness and concealment. For this reason, most of the beings one encounters in the *Imaginal* are individual souls, some of such antiquity that they stand like landmarks on the sweep of the regions: *a great mountain makes its own weather*.

Ultimately, awareness is the dream body—but it is *intent* that gives it coherence and provides its motive power. Training the intent is a matter of bringing awareness fully to bear with constancy of benevolence and absence of malevolence—what is called *sincerity*. This is the clearest focus of intent and serves as the foundation for all further elaborations. It is sometimes thought of as the practitioner's *pass*, that which allows one to move facilely and gracefully through the regions without creating friction, resistance or backlash.

When we consider how other beings in the *Imaginal* perceive us, we recall that within that realm we appear as a living image, a living symbol, just as do all the other beings there. Because of the archetypal nature of the dream space, and especially of the eight regions, all the symbol-beings appear as individual manifestations of eight archetypal orders of beings.

SUN	THE PIONEER
LAKE	THE MYSTIC
FIRE	THE TEACHER
LIGHTNING	THE TRICKSTER
WIND	THE HEALER
WATER	THE ARTIST
MOUNTAIN	THE DISSIDENT
MOON	THE MIDWIFE

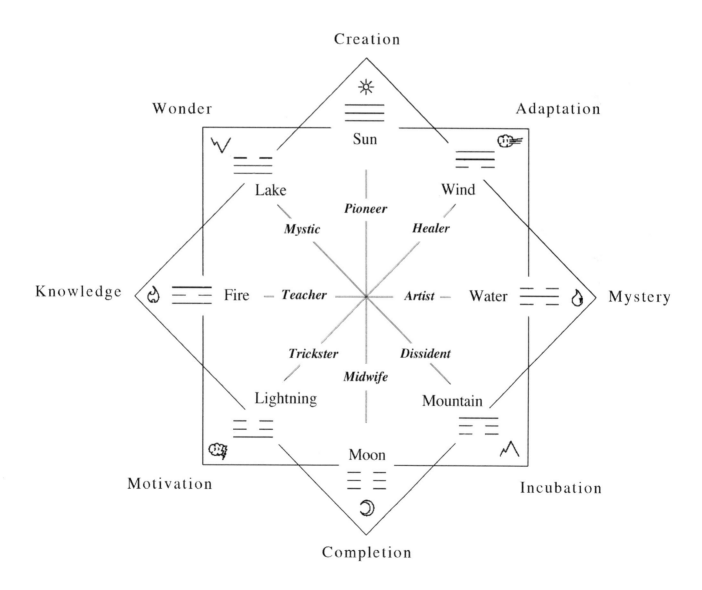

FIGURE 19: ARCHETYPES OF THE INNER COMPASS

Archetypes are broad classes of beings that find their manifestations in individuals, none of which can ever contain the entirety of the archetype. "Tree" is an archetype and no individual tree—oak or pine or apple or manzanita—ever fulfills the entire potential of its archetype, which includes all trees in all places in all times. Therefore:

> When we envision *The Pioneer*, what we really envision is *All Kinds of Pioneers*
>
> When we envision *The Mystic*, what we really envision is *All Kinds of Mystics*
>
> When we envision *The Teacher*, what we really envision is *All Kinds of Teachers*
>
> When we envision *The Trickster*, what we really envision is *All Kinds of Tricksters*
>
> When we envision *The Healer*, what we really envision is *All Kinds of Healers*
>
> When we envision *The Artist*, what we really envision is *All Kinds of Artists*
>
> When we envision *The Dissident*, what we really envision is *All Kinds of Dissidents*
>
> When we envision *The Midwife*, what we really envision is *All Kinds of Midwives*

The deeper one delves into each archetype, the more *kinds* reveal themselves.

> What different *kinds* of Pioneers are there?
>
> What different *kinds* have there ever been?
>
> What different *kinds* will there ever be?
>
> What characteristics do all the different *kinds* of Pioneers share?
>
> What preconceptions stand in the way of recognizing the different *kinds* of Pioneers?

Similar questions are asked of each of the archetypes, of course. Reflecting on the answers to these and further questions in regard to each of the eight archetypes opens up the heart-mind of the diviner-practitioner, allowing for a fuller recognition of the vast array of individual characteristics within an archetype. From this perspective, individuals manifest the different kinds of archetypes in the sprit of diversity, whereby every possibility is explored in the same way that a master musician will explore all the possible *variations on a theme*.

One way to consider all the different kinds of each archetype is to juxtapose each with all the possible combinations of archetypes, much as hexagrams are composed of upper and lower trigrams:

Pioneer of Pioneers	Pioneer of Mystics	Pioneer of Teachers	Pioneer of Tricksters
Mystic of Pioneers	Mystic of Mystics	Mystic of Teachers	Mystic of Tricksters
Teacher of Pioneers	Teacher of Mystics	Teacher of Teachers	Teacher of Tricksters
Trickster of Pioneers	Trickster of Mystics	Trickster of Teachers	Trickster of Tricksters
Healer of Pioneers	Healer of Mystics	Healer of Teachers	Healer of Tricksters
Artist of Pioneers	Artist of Mystics	Artist of Teachers	Artist of Tricksters
Dissident of Pioneers	Dissident of Mystics	Dissident of Teachers	Dissident of Tricksters
Midwife of Pioneers	Midwife of Mystics	Midwife of Teachers	Midwife of Tricksters

Pioneer of Healers	Pioneer of Artists	Pioneer of Dissidents	Pioneer of Midwives
Mystic of Healers	Mystic of Artists	Mystic of Dissidents	Mystic of Midwives
Teacher of Healers	Teacher of Artists	Teacher of Dissidents	Teacher of Midwives
Trickster of Healers	Trickster of Artists	Trickster of Dissidents	Trickster of Midwives
Healer of Healers	Healer of Artists	Healer of Dissidents	Healer of Midwives
Artist of Healers	Artist of Artists	Artist of Dissidents	Artist of Midwives
Dissident of Healers	Dissident of Artists	Dissident of Dissidents	Dissident of Midwives
Midwife of Healers	Midwife of Artists	Midwife of Dissidents	Midwife of Midwives

The possible permutations do not actually duplicate themselves here. *Pioneer of Mystics* is different than *Mystic of Pioneers*. *Teacher of Midwives* is different than *Midwife of Teachers*. *Artist of Dissidents* is different than *Dissident of Artists*.

As Figure 19, above, shows, there is a direct correlation between each region, its attribute, and its archetype:

SUN	CREATION	PIONEER
LAKE	WONDER	MYSTIC
FIRE	KNOWLEDGE	TEACHER
LIGHTNING	MOTIVATION	TRICKSTER
WIND	ADAPTATION	HEALER
WATER	MYSTERY	ARTIST
MOUNTAIN	INCUBATION	DISSIDENT
MOON	COMPLETION	MIDWIFE

In other words, the Sun region is the dwelling place of the Pioneer archetype. *All Kinds of Pioneers*, moreover, points to the eight archetypal *kinds* of Pioneers within the Sun region: Pioneer of Pioneers, Mystic of Pioneers, Teacher of Pioneers, Trickster of Pioneers, Healer of Pioneers, Artist of Pioneers, Dissident of Pioneers, and Midwife of Pioneers. Obviously, the same *variations of a theme* approach applies to each of the other regions.

Within the fluidity of the *formative substance* of the dream space, diviner-practitioners can find themselves disoriented if they possess no ordering principle to apply to the *Imaginal*. The unitary nature of non-duality provides the ultimate experience of perfect communion, which is the ideal state of stillness and nondifferentiation from which all one's actions ought originate. Moving into the state of acting, however, requires borders and differentiations in order to apply one's intent with efficacy. The ordering principle of the archetypes is organic, in the sense that it is part and parcel of the same pattern of perception intrinsic to the *formative substance* and its manifestations.

One's dream body, then, appears to other beings within the *Imaginal* as one of the possible kinds of one of the archetypes. Similarly, the dream bodies of other beings within the *Imaginal* appear to oneself as one of the possible kinds of one of the archetypes. And, likewise, the regions themselves appear to each dream body as one of the possible kinds of their respective archetype.

Crystalizing one's own symbology as a living image brings one's dream body into sharper focus for all to recognize. Sharpening one's own focus on the recognizable characteristics of other living images and regions brings one into attunement with all in the dream space. This attunement of the dream body to the dream space is the secret path to attracting great-souled allies in one's quest to marshal the *formative substance* into manifestations of universal benefit.

CONCLUSION

"What is essential to understand," my teacher Robert Sharp used to say, "is that there is a real world on the other side of this one and that there is an ancient lineage of savants dedicated to opening the gate of immortality that stands between them."[29]

"Think about all the great-souled ones who have lived and died," my teacher Master Khigh Alx Dhiegh used to say. "Can we not hear them at our elbow, whispering to us warnings and promises in order to bring the great dream of the ancients to realization? Is that not what we ourselves will do when we pass over to the other side and see the living in need of truth? When did people stop listening to spirit? When did people stop seeing themselves as a bridge between the past and the future?"

"All this is already dying," my teacher Don Alfredo used to say, motioning to the wilderness of the Barranca del Cobre. "We have held the outside world away from us as long as we can and we can feel it at the edges now. It will arrive soon but when it does, we will not be here. We will have already entered that other place where we cannot be touched."

The common trait that great teachers exhibit is *reverence*. Reverence for all life and all spirit and especially for their own precious lifetimes. To safeguard what is nearest—that is the secret. That is the source of *intimacy* that spills out into the world and benefits the furthest reaches of Creation. Like the heart pumping blood to the extremities, the benevolent soul sends blessings to all the immortal relationships between all the mortal things in Creation.

The base of the pyramid is its *perfectibility*. The capstone of the pyramid is its *magnanimity*. Each stone of the pyramid is the *collective intent* of Human Nature to allow the world of manifestation to reflect the beauty, truth and symmetry of the spirit world. The pyramid is our collective work, the raising of the Golden Age of Humanity—work that cannot be accomplished solely in the world of the five senses, but needs be guided by the collective dream body of Human Nature.

Which brings us inevitability to the MOON of COMPLETION and the close of this little work in the form of several aphorisms celebrating the tradition of rational-mysticism:

---

[29] See my *In the Oneness of Time* and *Way of the Diviner*.

I. THE OPEN SECRET

The One *is* Everything

The One embodies its own Duality

Every Individual within the One embodies the same Unitary Duality

Matter *is* Spirit

II. REPOLARIZATION

The creative moment is the life-changing moment

The creative life is the ecstatic life

Perfect equilibrium is perfect ecstasy

Equilibrium requires that sooner or later, everything turns into its opposite

Sometimes intention must occupy one extreme in order to bring about the other

Change never favors individuals, but is always a redistribution of energy within the Whole

Change is the cause, not the effect

Change is the medium of transmutation

III. EMBODIED CHANGE

It is not often an enlightened being emerges from the uninitiated masses—

and even less often that the enlightened being remains among the masses,

like a wave collapsing back into the sea,

eschewing the cocoon encapsulating others in the trappings of specialness:

Without changing a single thing about yourself,

be that person.

IV. EMBODIED SPACE

Awaken early,

Find lifelong allies.

Afterword

The greatest tragedy in life is to arrive at someone else's destination

I was walking along a broad, level road in the company of great-souled allies, laughing and joking in that relaxed way only boon companions do. The cobblestoned road ran straight and true towards the gleaming spires rising above the lush rainforest that reached right up to the edge of the raised highway. A splash of color down below caught my eye and, stepping off the road and sliding down the embankment to pick the flower, I called over my shoulder to my kindred spirits, "I'll be right back!"

That's how I found myself here, wherever here is. In the body of a nineteen year old boy with no self-discipline or sense of the common good. I've been here, wherever here is, now for 48 years and would like to think this body is the better for my influence. I do know for certain that I am the better for its influence on me, for there is nothing in Creation like awakened mortality to remind the soul of the long ascent out of darkness into light.

Now, I don't know how you got here, wherever here is. And I don't know what kind of body you found yourself in then. Or what influence you've had on it in the meantime. But I do know for certain that its influence on you is profound, a kaleidoscope of paradoxical moments strung like pearls to treasure for the grace and nobility they have bestowed.

As for my own destination, I have simply looked for what has been left undone by those who came before and pointed to uncharted terrains for those who come after. It is a path that has always proven to carry me deeper into the mysteries than I would have ever dared imagine. I have, of course, seen along the way the terrible grief laid at the feet of so many who deserved so much better. On the other hand, I have been fortunate to love greatly and be loved greatly and, trite as it sounds to the modern mind, there is nothing so treasured in the vault of the ancient soul.

These days, as the end nears, I can feel myself already clambering back up the embankment, clutching this golden flower in one hand and waving a greeting with the other, unscathed. But not untouched.

3 + 4 :: 6 + 1 :: RETURN

Delicias, Winter 2017

SCHOOL OF RATIONAL MYSTICISM

DIVINATION:

The Toltec I Ching
    with Martha Ramirez-Oropeza
In the Oneness of Time: The Education of a Diviner
Way of the Diviner

RESEARCHES ON THE TOLTEC I CHING:

Vol. 1. *I Ching Mathematics: The Science of Change*
Vol. 2. *The Image and Number Treatise: The Oracle and the War on Fate*
Vol. 3. *The Forest of Fire Pearls Oracle: The Medicine Warrior I Ching*
Vol. 4. *I Ching Mathematics for the King Wen Version*
Vol. 5. *Why Study the I Ching? A Brief Course in the Direct Seeing of Reality*
Vol. 6. *The Open Secret I Ching: The Diviner's Journey and the Road of Freedom*
Vol. 7. *The Alchemical I Ching: 64 Keys to the Secret of Internal Transmutation*
Vol. 8. *intrachange: I Ching Chess*

SELF-REALIZATION PRACTICES:

The Five Emanations: Aligning the Modern Mind with the Ancient Soul
The Spiritual Basis of Good Fortune: Retracing the Ancient Path of Personal Transformation
Facing Light: Preparing for the Moment of Dying
The Soul of Power: Deconstructing the Art of War
The Tao of Cool: Deconstructing the Tao Te Ching
Fragments of Anamnesia
We Are I Am: Visions of Mystical Union

MISCELLANEOUS

POETRY:
Palimpsest Flesh

NOVEL:
Life and Death in the Hotel Bardo

Made in the USA
San Bernardino, CA
25 October 2018